Bedtime Stories for Kids

2 in 1: An Amazing Collection of Meditation Stories to Put Your Children and Toddlers to Sleep. Teach Them Mindfulness with These Tales About Unicorns, Dinosaurs and Dragons

Ingrid Connor

Table of Contents

Bedtime Stories for Kids -1- 7

Introduction 8

Chapter 1: Hector the Brave, a Knight in Pyjamas.............. 10

Chapter 2: The Magic carpet Ride.................................... 16

Chapter 3: Scrambled Eggs and Jam 22

Chapter 4: The Ducks and the Dog................................ 28

Chapter 5: What can the Weatherman do?...................... 34

Chapter 6: The day Johnny went bananas 40

Chapter 7: Double Vision 46

Chapter 8: Grandma's most unusual knitting pattern 52

Chapter 9: An Afternoon with an Alien 58

Chapter 10: Beyond the Clouds 64

Chapter 11: The Mysterious Tunnel 71

Chapter 12: Grandpa's Magic Motor bike 77

Chapter 13: Message in a bottle 83

Chapter 14: Ronnie and the Marathon run 89

Chapter 15: Simon the boy who loved Science.................. 96

Chapter 16: Dad favorite party tricks 102

Chapter 17: Mission Submersible 109

Chapter 18: The Runaway Kite..................................115

Chapter 19: The most unusual rescue story 120

Chapter 20: Down a rabbit hole 126

Conclusion 133

Bedtime Stories For Kids -2- 135

Introduction 136

Chapter 1: Sammy's Space Adventure 138

Chapter 2: Amy's New Friends.................................145

Chapter 3: What lies behind the rainbow?.....................152

Chapter 4: The little dinosaur that couldn't sleep...........157

Chapter 5: The boy who spoke to animals......................163

Chapter 6: The Secret Treehouse 170

Chapter 7: The Land of Magical Creatures 177

Chapter 8: Molly in the Candyland............................184

Chapter 9: Kitty's Way Home 190

Chapter 10: Jimmy's Good Deeds 197

Chapter 11: In the toy chest 203

Chapter 12: How Jackson Saved Winter 209

Chapter 13: How Cody Met Superheroes.........................215

Chapter 14: Charlie's night at the supermarket...............221

Chapter 15: A day at the beach...............................226

Chapter 16: Sarah and the Fairies 232

Chapter 17: Billy and the Pirates.................................238

Chapter 18: Adam's New Friend 243

Chapter 19: Bella's and Star's Adventure.......................249

Chapter 20: Leilani's Adventure in the Jungle 255

Conclusion 260

Bedtime Stories for Kids -1-

A Unique Short Fairy Tales Collection for Children to Help them Fall Asleep Fast. Have a Relaxing Night's Sleep with Lovely Dreams and Moral Stories. Easy to Read for All Ages

Ingrid Connor

Introduction

Children are little bubbles of limitless energy. It's unexpected how even after a long, eventful day, they are full of energy during the night, playing and running around. They can be up and keep you up with them. Maybe sometimes, a few mistimed naps help with that. But after a long, tiring day, when all we long for is a break and a peaceful sleep, even we often manage to stay up for a long while. So, just putting them to bed and expecting them to fall asleep might not always work out.

This is where a bed-time routine filled with simple yet fantastic tales, come in handy. Don't let them sleep to the thought of the fight they had with their sibling or friend. Let them fall asleep thinking of a certain Elephant named Joey, or a Panda named Red, from a beautiful imaginary land. For bedtime stories help calm their rushing minds, help them relax, and reduce any stress. And above all, it helps them imagine. Imagination helps them to create and to dream.

Bedtime stories become door to a world of knowledge, which opens them up to many more worlds. Their developing brains listen to these bedtime tales and start storing ideas. They start understanding consequences, and they start drawing up their own endings. The next time you are telling your child a bedtime story, they might even surprise you by predicting the right one.

Bedtime stories can help instill much-needed values. They can send your child to a beautiful, dreamy world. They can teach your child mindfulness. And after all, who doesn't love a good story. It might even help you relax and give you, your much-needed distraction.

Bedtime stories are mostly moralizing. They become instrumental in helping your children grow. Fiction is only an exaggerated reality. When you tell them the story of the boy who cried wolf, they think twice before lying when they do something naughty, which to me, is a parenting win.

Chapter 1: Hector the Brave, a Knight in Pyjamas

Hector had always wanted to be a knight. He had dreams of being a knight, he read stories about knights and he listened to his brothers talk about being a knight. Hector was the youngest boy in his family and all his brothers were knights. Sadly Hector was still too young to be a knight.

"Knights have to be big and strong," said his eldest brother, Igor.

"Knights have to wear heavy armour," said his middle brother, Warwick.

"Knights have to ride horses very fast and fight fierce dragons," said his next in line brother, Harold.

Poor Hector just sighed and wondered if he would <u>ever</u> be big enough to be a real knight.

Just then his mum called him to the kitchen. Hector shuffled along and dragged his heels. He was feeling very discouraged. Hector had to help his mum carry water from the well to the kitchen. When Hector huffed and puffed about doing this his mum squeezed the muscles on his arms.

"Hector," his mum said, "these little pumpkin pips need to grow into big muscles if you ever want to be a brave knight in shining armour. Come on, carry the water bucket and fetch the water and your muscles will grow big and strong, just like your brothers."

Mum smiled at Hector, her youngest little warrior, who was so desperate to be a knight and wear shining armour like his brothers.

Hector fetched the water and then sat outside under a tree to dream about being a famous knight. While he was dreaming he saw himself fighting battles alongside his brothers. He saw himself on a great white charger racing down the hillside holding the banner and being the bravest knight of all. He saw the colourful plumes on the knights helmet waving in the wind showing how mighty he was.

Suddenly Hector woke up to the sound of the knights returning to the village. Everyone ran out to meet them including Hector. The girls had baskets of flowers to throw at the feet of the knights as they were such heroes. Hector didn't want to throw flowers, that would be too silly for him. He felt something hit him on the back of the head. It was a bunch of flowers. Yuk, thought Hector and he turned round to see who had thrown flowers at him.

It was Camilla from next door and she was teasing him.

"Come on Sir Hector the brave, where is your horse today?" she said as she threw another flower at the very cross 'wanna be' knight, Hector.

Hector was furious and marched back home. When he got to the door his brothers were waiting. They ruffled his hair and a whole lot of petals fell to the ground.

"Hello little brother," they said. "Wearing flowers in your hair today?"

The big brave knights went inside the house to take off their armour and rest after their busy ride.

Hector watched and wished he could be like them. They laughed and joked about their day out fighting dragons and keeping everyone safe. They took off their armour and left it in the trophy room. It was a room full of their prizes at jousting competitions.

That night when everyone had gone to bed Hector decided he would creep into the room where the knights hung up their armour. He slipped out of bed wearing his pyjamas. He did not want to put on his slippers so he could tiptoe really quietly out into the hall and down to the trophy room.

"I just want to see how heavy a helmet is and if my muscles are growing just a little bit," said Hector to himself.

He tiptoed quietly along the passage and into the room full of the knight's special armour. He felt a bit scared as he came face to face with their empty helmets. He saw the bright feathers waving gently as he came close to the helmets. They were called plumes and every helmet had one. Each of his brothers had a full suit of armour and each suit of armour had a different coloured plume on the helmet. A bright feather plume was a sign of bravery and strength. The more plumes a knight had earned the more brave deeds he had done.

Hector's brothers had told Hector when he became a knight he would earn plumes for all the brave deeds he had done. Hector looked at his brothers helmets and saw they all had plumes. He saw his youngest brother's helmet sitting on the floor. It was the smallest helmet and had the smallest plume. Hector wondered if it would fit him. He decided to try it on.

He lifted the helmet carefully off the floor and slowly put it on his head. It was heavy, but Hector was determined to try and at least wear the helmet. He was just getting used to the weight of the helmet when he heard a strange noise outside. It was a sort of scuffling, snorting noise. Slowly Hector stood up and looked outside to see what it could be. When he tried to look out the window it was dark, very dark. Something was blocking the window and he couldn't see what it was.

The helmet was heavy and a bit too big for Hector. It made him feel a little dizzy, but he tried to stand up and see how it felt to be wearing a real knights helmet. When he finally got his balance he turned to look out of the window. It was at that moment his eyes met the eyes of the dragon. Big staring googly eyes. Dark eyes with shades of firey orange like flashing flames. Hector got such a fright he took a step backwards away from the window.

In a split second he knocked over the first suit of armour. The first suit knocked over the second suit of armour and that suit knocked over the third and biggest suit of armour.

Hector got such a fright he lost his balance and crashed to the floor in amongst all the suits of armour. The helmet he was wearing slipped over his one eye and he found himself sitting on the floor holding one of the heavy gloves that the knights have to wear. He had knocked over all the suits of armour.

Crash, bang, smash! What a terrible noise it all made.

The dragon, creeping past the house got a firht too! The dragon saw the helmet and then heard the noise of the crashing armour. It sounded as if all the knights in the village were after him. The dragon turned tail and disappeared. The dragon disappeared so fast there was only a puff of smile left hanging outside the window.

Hector was left sitting on the floor with the helmet on the wrong way round. He was stunned for a moment and forgot where he was. He looked around and then he remembered he had seen a dragon and the dragon had run away. Hector was about to get up and untangle himself from the armour and tiptoe back to bed.

There was no chance that Hector could just creep to bed. No he had set off the alarm and suddenly his brothers burst into the room ready to defend the house from the fierce dragon. They saw little Hector sitting on the floor in his pyjamas, with a helmet slipping off his head. Hector was not quite sure what had happened for a moment and then he felt very embarrassed as his brothers started laughing at him. Laughing, but clapping at the same time.

"Bravo bravo, Hector," they cheered.

"Well done, Hector," they said in their big voices. "You chased away a dragon, that was very brave."

Hector tried to stand up, but as he did the helmet fell off his head and clattered to the floor.

He thought his brothers would be cross, but they carried on laughing.

"Oh, Hector the Protector," they said. "You are the first knight in pyjamas to scare a dragon and protect his family! "

Hector looked up and felt proud for a moment. Then he saw his brothers were still laughing.

"Can I be a knight now?" he asked.

"A knight in pyjamas," laughed his brothers. "No little brother you have a bit more growing up to do, but well done you did protect us. Keep trying hard to get big and strong and brave too.

Then Hector's mum came round the corner. She had heard all the noise and wanted to know what wasall the fuss about. Hector's brothers explained that Hector had been a hero and chased a dragon away. Mum was so proud she gave Hector a big hug to say well done.

Hector was embarrassed about his pyjamas.

"A brave brave knight in pyjamas," said his mum.

Hectors brothers bowed to the knight in pyjamas and Hector felt happy as he went to bed.

Chapter 2: The Magic carpet Ride

John loved his father very much. He was so proud of him because he was a doctor. John's father helped people get better and he was a very good doctor. John watched his father leave the house early in the morning and come back late at night. Every time his father went to work he would bring John another new toy or game or smart clothes.

"Here you are my boy," he would say, "this is something to make you happy."

John used to put the new things in his room, but he really wanted to spend time with his father.

John's mom would tell him how busy doctors were and what good work they did, but John just did not understand and he felt angry. One day he stamped his feet and decided he was going to run away, but before he left he wanted to follow his father and see what he did every day.

John watched his father get ready for work. John saw a truck parked in the street. He had seen this truck before and the man who drove it used to wave to John. John never waved back because he was always cross. He saw his father driving off every day and so why would he want to wave and be happy. The man waved at John's mom and she always waved back.

"Ha," said John, in a cross voice. "I don't want to be friendly."

John went inside to play with his new toys, but he did not feel happy.

He watched the truck as the truck arrived every day and he saw his father get into the truck and drive off out of town.

The next day, when the truck arrived, John looked out of the window. He saw the man waving and waiting. He crept around the side of the house and behind a bush and then he jumped into the back of the truck. It was full of rolled up carpets so John wriggled inside one of the carpets. He felt quite excited about this adventure. He heard the driver come to close the back of the truck and say hi to his dad. Then the truck started and off they went. John was so happy that at last he would get to see where his dad went and why this truck took him away from home every day.

John snuggled into the rolled up carpet and soon the noise of the truck, and the movement along the road, sent him off to sleep. He began to dream. John had a strange dream about a magic carpet ride. In his dream the carpet he was rolled up in began to unroll and lift up out of the truck. John hung on to the sides and watched as the carpet carried him over the town and out into the country. The carpet ride took John on a long journey in his dream. He floated away across the town and he drifted over different houses. Sometimes, along the way John saw poor families struggling to have enough food on the table. Not everyone had nice toys like John did. John wanted to reach out and help them everyone but the carpet did not stop and John felt it take off and ride away again.

Finally John felt the carpet stop. He felt a bump and opened his eyes. It was dark inside the truck and he realised that he had been asleep. The carpet ride had been a dream. Here he was and the truck doors began to open. John wondered what he was going to see. He wondered if he was still dreaming. Suddenely he heard his father's voice. He tried to peep out of the carpet ut it was rolled up inside the truck.

John was pleased he had heard his father's voice. He did not want to show himself until he could be sure it was safe to do so. An old man came out of the farm house. John could see everyone knew each other. They were friends. Then the front door of the farm house burst open and lots of children came out to greet everyone. They were very excited, John heard them chattering and laughing. They knew there was something special about this truck. John felt happy when he heard the excited children. He wondered why they were so pleased to see this truck.

The truck driver went to the back of the truck and took out a big box. John stayed hidden in the rolled up carpet. The driver carried the box to the house and the children followed happily behind him. John saw his father walking with the children too. John wanted to follow everyone, but he was afraid that his father would be upset that John had hidden in the back of the truck. The driver came back to the truck and John held his breath as the driver reached into the truck ad lifted the carpet out of the back. The carpet that John was rolled up in!

John felt the carpet moving! He pinched himself! Was this another dream! The carpet lifted out of the truck and was carried inside the farm house. The driver grunted and said something about how heavy this carpet was. He took the carpet inside and laid id down on the floor.

"Look what we have bought you today,' said his father.

"A nice, big carpet for the children to play on," added the truck driver. "It is big and fluffy and much heavier than I remember but I will roll it out for you all to see."

John felt himself being lifted up and swung around. Then he felt himself land on the floor and slowly the carpet was unrolled.

The truck driver rolled the carpet carefully onto the floor. What a surprise everyone got. The carpet unrolled and with it a small boy cmae rolling out onto the floor.

There was silence in the room. John looked up and saw his father's face looking down at him.

"John," shouted his father." What are you doing here?"

John could not say a word. He just sat there staring up with big brown eyes looking at everyone in the room. He did not know what his father would do next.

Suddenly everyone began to laugh at the boy who had rolled out of the carpet.

Slowly John stood up feeling a bit shaky. His father ran towards him and gave him a big hug.

"My boy'" his father said. "Are you alright?"

Everyone was looking at the little boy who had by magic it seemed just rolled out of a carpet. How did he get there, and where did he come from?

John decided to smile and that set everyone off laughing and smiling at the boy who had rolled out of the carpet. John told his dad all about how he wanted to see what his dad was doing and so he had followed him in the truck.

"It was like a magic carpet ride, Dad," said John. He explained to his dad how he had felt as he ws flying through the air on a magic carpet. While he flew he saw houses and people down below and then suddenely the ride ended right here outside a large farm house.

John's dad explained that he came here to help these families who did not have as much as other families. Dad and the truck driver were part of an organisation helping others have a better life, especially the needy children. So they bought food parcels and toys for the children. This week they had been given a carpet to bring for the farm house where the children lived.

"Oh Dad, that is so special. I am glad I know why you spend so much time away from home," said John. His dad smiled and hugged John again. He knew he should have told John before but now this was indeed a magical moment for them both.

"I am so happy that you are here too John," said his dad. The children came running across the carpet to get to know John. John loved meeeting all these happy children and sharing in their laughter as they opend the parcels the truck driver took out of the back of the truck. John helped his dad and the truck driver to carrythe toys and the food parcels inside for the children.

John saw the real happiness on the faces of the children and how good it was to be there with his dad.his father helped every day. John asked his dad if he could be part of the magic carpet ride again and his dd said he would be so happy to have John on his team.

What a wonderful day! John rode home with his dad and he knew he would never forget he had been on a truly magical carpet ride.

Chapter 3: Scrambled Eggs and Jam

Michael and his brother Luke were so excited. Their dad was taking them away on a camping trip.

"Now boys," said dad. "It is very important to be prepared on these camping trips. The boys nodded. They knew their dad was always super organised and he would have everything listed and checked and double checked before they left.

Mom helped to pack the van and make sure the boys had all they needed for a camping holiday. It was just for the weekend, but there seemed to be a lot of 'stuff'. Mom and her girl friends were going away to a spa for some pampering. The boys, and dad included, had turned their noses up at any thought of pampering.

"We are going to rough it right out there in the bush," said dad as he packed the basics.

"A tent to sleep in and a camp fire to cook our food. Just a frying pan and a kettle and that is all we will need," dad said to the boys. Mom packed all the food they would need and she even gave dad a menu of meals to prepare.

"Campers!" called dad. With that dad blew on his whistle and the boys knew it was time to fall in with dad, who had been a scout when he was younger.

Finally, the camper van got going and the boys looked out the back window to see mom waving and getting smaller and smaller in the distance. Dad was so happy to be taking the boys out on a camping trip. The boys were a bit worried about his 'Texas Ranger' attitude and over excitement to get to the camp site.

"You are going to love this," said dad.

The boys looked at each other and hoped they would. Two nights away from home and mom's delicious cooking. That could be a bit of a problem, but the boys had stocked up with some really useful snacks and a large bag of popcorn for emergencies.

At last they reached the camp site. Dad parked the van and walked around looking for a suitable spot to set up the tent. Finally he came back to the van and told the boys he would drive a bit further down the track and stop in a clearing at the bottom of the track under a large, shady tree. It looked good. They put the tent up next to the camper van and dad handed out some snacks for supper.

"We'll cook properly in the morning boys," said dad. "It's getting a bit late and I see there are some rain clouds over head."

The boys looked up and sure enough it did look like rain. Dad wanted to sleep in the tent. The boys thought it would be a good idea to sleep in the back of the van.

"Come on, where's your sense of adventure?" asked dad as he set out his sleeping bag and crawled into the tent. It was the first time he had used the tent in many years.

"This tent has a history. My dad took us camping in this trusty, old tent," said dad as he started to set up the tent he had borrowed from Gramps.

"Yeh, this old tent has done the rounds. My dad used it for camping and we took it to the scout jamboree," said dad with glee.

The boys looked at each other with a quizzical look. What on earth was a jamboree? They decided not to ask because they didn't really feel like one of dad's explanations.

Dad was flapping around with ground sheets and tent flaps and zippers and all sorts of bits and pieces. Eventually he seemed to have the tent sorted. The boys watched from the safety of the camper van. They were all grateful for an early night and as they got into bed the boys looked out of the window. There was a distant sound of thunder and then some rain came down. The boys went to sleep.

During the night it began to rain harder. The rain started to run down the track making a little river. A little river of mud. The muddy river ran down towards the big tree and the clearing where the boys and their dad were camping. The boys continued to sleep happily in the camper van. Dad rolled over in his sleeping bag. He heard a strange noise, a sort of squishy noise. He lent over from his sleeping bag and touched something wet and cold. What was it dad wondered?

Dad found his torch and switched it on. Oh my goodness, what a fright he got. The little muddy river flowing down the track had seeped under his tent and round his sleeping bag.   The tent was like a pond and dad felt as if he was floating in the middle of it on his sleeping bag. A hole in the corner revealed the place where the water had crept in and filled the ground sheet.

Dad crept out of the tent and knocked on the van door. He was soaking wet and so was his sleeping bag. He looked like a drowned rat!

Michael and Luke were surprised to see their dad standing out in the rain. They offered him blankets and dad settled down on the front seat for the rest of the night.

In the morning the boys looked around for their dad. He was awake and up early before anyone else. He had opened up the box of goodies mom had packed. Dad was waving a frying pan around and getting ready to make a super, duper breakfast. He blew on his whistle like a camp ranger and was ready for a brisk hike and then to cook breakfast.

Michael and Luke pretended to be enthusiastic as they followed their dad out of the camp. They looked briefly behind them to see stacked up around the camp fire area were piles of wood, boxes of cooking utensils and the breakfast they were looking forward to. Bacon and fried eggs with fresh toast and jam. It was going to be yummy.

Actually the boys wondered why they had to go on a hike. Why not just skip straight to breakfast. Dad was determined that they would all be good scouts and have a healthy walk and then a healthy breakfast. There was no point in arguing with dad.

"Hikers!" he called out as he took hold of his hiking stick and set off up the path into the woods.

The boys tumbled out of the camper van. They put on their hiking boots and got ready to follow dad. There was a short trail up the side of the camp and back again. Fortunately it was not to far and well signposted so they did not get lost.

"Right boys, follow me back to camp and watch me whip up a fantastic, world class campers' breakfast!" exclaimed dad enthusiastically.

Dad delegated chores to be done to get ready for breakfast.

Light the fire, sort out the plates and get the frying pan. Put on the kettle for tea.

Dad reached for the box of eggs and gave Michael the frying pan.

"Hold onto this Michael while I sort out the eggs," said dad taking charge of breakfast.

Dad stepped towards the fire ready to crack the eggs and start his world famous breakfast. The boys held their breath. They watched dad lift up the box of eggs. Then, almost in slow motion it seemed, he tripped on a tree root and the eggs flew up into the air. Dad had a look of shock and horror on his face as half a dozen eggs were airborne.

It was Michael to the rescue. He held out the frying pan and caught the eggs as they came tumbling down. There was the awful sound of eggs cracking and at the same time a groan from dad.

Michael checked on the eggs and Luke lifted his dad up off the ground.

Dad looked at the frying pan. There would be no fried eggs this morning.

"Don't worry," said the boys we can pick out the bits of shell and scrambled eggs will be just as delicious.

"Scrambled eggs and Jam," said Luke with a smile.

"Tell us about a Jam-boree while we have this world class, scrambled egg breakfast," said Michael.

It was a way of getting dad to recover from his mishap. Dad dusted himself off. He looked pleased about telling the boys about his scout camping, jamboree days.

Dad and the boys headed home the next day. Dad told mum about the scrambled eggs and Jam. Mum scrunched up her nose a first, but dad explained that they didn't EAT scrambled eggs and jam They just had good fun and laughed about dad's Jamboree days. They had eaten a world class scrambled egg breakfast. Dad made a mental note to speak to Gramps about his leaky tent!

Chapter 4: The Ducks and the Dog

Danny Boy was a golden retriever who lived on a farm with his family, the Sutherlands. Mr Sutherland loved his farm and the apples he grew in his orchard. He walked down to the orchard every day to check on his beautiful fruit trees. Danny Boy always went with him. Mr Sutherland, John, loved to whistle or sing a tune called Danny Boy, it was his favorite song. That was why his dog was named Danny Boy.

At the end of the orchard was a dam and after their walk together Danny Boy always went for a swim in the dam. John would throw sticks for Danny Boy to retrieve and Danny Boy would love pleasing his master by diving into the water and fetching the stick. Danny Boy held his head up high out of the water and swam back to give the stick to John. They had such happy times together.

There was a family of ducks living on the dam and they would quack and make a big fuss when Danny Boy came near their side of the dam. Sometimes, if John forgot to throw the stick for Danny Boy, his attention would turn to the ducks! Mrs Duck was very protective of her little brood of ducklings. Five little ducklings that swam around the dam after Mrs Duck. If Danny Boy started to look playfully at Mrs Duck she would quickly tell him off. Mrs Duck would make some very sharp quacks and swim away with her little ones following her.

"Come on Danny Boy. Its home we go," called John as he turned back to get home in time for dinner. Danny Boy was eager to follow his master. He knew there was sure to be a juicy bone waiting at home for a well behaved dog.

This was the pattern of Danny Boy and John's life every day. Together they enjoyed the walk and the run back home after chasing sticks. Until one day something changed and Danny Boy found himself trapped. He had swum in the dam as usual, and he had fetched sticks as usual, but then John was distracted and busy on his phone. John threw the stick for Danny Boy into a reed bank and without thinking Danny Boy dived into the reeds to fetch his stick. He did not see the tangled fishing line in amongst the reeds. He tried to fetch the stick, but his nose was stuck in the mess of fishing line.

He heard John calling him. Danny Boy wanted to answer, but because his nose was tangled, his bark to say 'Here I am,' did not come out loud enough. He tried to wriggle out of the reeds, but the more he wriggled, the worse his situation became. Then he heard John shout for the last time.

"Danny Boy, here Danny Boy. Come on boy, or have you gone home already?" shouted John.

 John started to walk back home thinking that while he had been on the phone Danny Boy had decided to go home. Danny Boy had not gone home, he was stuck in the dam.

When John arrived home he expected Danny Boy to come racing out of the house to cover him in licks and wag his tail super fast. Danny Boy did not come running out to greet John. John walked round the house calling. John went back to the orchard, but Danny boy did not come running out to greet him. John went home feeling sad. He said he was going to search again in the morning.

Danny Boy lay shivering in the dam. Luckily the tangle of reeds kept him afloat. He thought if he could just get through the night John would find him. Just then he heard a funny swishing noise and he wondered what it was. The reeds started to move a little and then he heard a familiar quack and something prodded him in the back. Another quack came out and he felt another prod. He looked up through the reeds. What a lovely surprise he got. The duck family had swum over to the reeds. They were busy with their beaks tugging and pulling at the fishing line. Danny Boy kept really still and waited to see what was going to happen next. A wiggle here and another wiggle there and suddenly Danny Boy was free!

Mrs Duck waggled her tail in delight and Danny Boy wagged his tail back at her. He was free to run home. He ran as fast as he could along the path, through the orchard, and up to the back door. He scratched loudly on the door.

John opened the door and Danny Boy leaped into the kitchen. He actually knocked John over with his excitement. Danny Boy's tail wagged like a helicopter taking off! John gave him lots of cuddles as well as a good rub down. Danny Boy was not able to tell John how he had managed to get out of a difficult situation. Danny Boy hoped that when he got back to the dam the next day he would be able to thank the ducks. He wasn't sure what he would do, but he knew he would not be chasing ducks tomorrow.

Danny Boy and John arrived at the dam the next day. Danny Boy knew he would not be swimming amongst the reeds. He waited for John to find a stick and throw it across the dam. John threw the stick across the dam, but Danny Boy hesitated. Something was wrong. Where was Mrs Duck and her ducklings? The dam was empty.

Danny Boy looked at John and then he looked at the stick floating on the dam. Danny Boy did not jump in to fetch the stick. He looked at John again and John just shook his head. He did not know what Danny Boy was trying to say. Danny Boy took off at top speed and ran round the dam. He ran round sniffing and snuffling everywhere. Then he ran back to John as if to say, come with me John!

John followed Danny Boy and wondered why he was not jumping into the dam to fetch his stick. Something was wrong. John shook his head and looked around. There were some car tracks leading up to the dam. He wondered where they came from. Danny Boy began to run in the direction of the tracks. They led away from the dam and up the hill.

John was getting quite out of breath and Danny Boy had his nose to the ground as he followed the tracks. Then Danny Boy stopped suddenly. He stood in front of a green feather lying in the grass. Danny Boy sniffed the air and looked round as if to tell John to hurry up and follow him. Danny Boy was heading towards the farmhouse on the top of a hill. He stopped again as he saw another feather, it was a duck's feather.

Danny Boy crouched down as he got closer to the farm house. John did the same as they came near to a shed at the back of the farmyard. Then Danny Boy stopped in his tracks and looked up to John. John crept to the window and looked inside the shed. Oh dear, oh dear. John shook his head and signalled to Danny Boy to stay down.

It was the duck family, captured by poachers and locked in cages in the shed. The poor ducks did not know what to do. Danny Boy nudged John's hand as if to urge him to do something. John nodded and crept round to the front of the shed. The door was open and so without waiting for a moment John rushed inside the shed and grabbed the cage holding the ducks.

No one saw John run into the shed, and out again, with the duck family. He ran back down to the dam and Danny Boy ran after him. When they got to the dam they opened the cage and Mrs Duck and her ducklings flew out and dived into the water. What a lot of quacking and tail wagging there was. Mrs Duck did some special duck dives as if to say thank you to Danny Boy and John. The little ducklings swan round in a circle and quacked and splashed too.

Danny Boy barked at the ducks and wagged his tail and John looked on and laughed. Imagine a dog and the ducks trying to talk to one another. John had no idea what they were saying, but it was obvious they were all happy that day. If Danny boy had been able to talk he probably would have said:

"One good turn deserves another."

Now Danny boy never chases the ducks and the ducks quack very happily when Danny Boy and John come down to the dam. It's just the place for a dog and some ducks.

Chapter 5: What can the Weatherman do?

Walter was the weatherman at the news station. It was his job to bring the weather to the people watching the news channel. Walter loved being the weatherman. He had a big map to point to various areas in the country. Walter liked to dress up to suit the weather. If it was going to be sunny he wore a big sun hat. If it was rainy, he wore his raincoat. When winter came Walter took out his woolly hat and a scarf. Walter just loved being the weatherman.

One day, when he looked at the weather report, all he saw was grey clouds. In fact there had been an unusual amount of grey clouds for the whole week. Walter could not wear his sunny outfits or his rainy outfits. He had no choice, he had to find grey clothes to wear. His grey clothes showed the viewers of his weather program that it was going to be a very grey, dismal weather report.

Walter did not know what to say to the weather channel. No sun, no rain, no wind, nothing to report just grey skies. It was so dull. Walter just shook his head and tried to think of what he could say to improve the weather report. He decided to go home early that day as there was no interesting weather. He left the weather station and walked home through the park. Walter sat on a bench in the park and closed his eyes to try and think about how he could brighten up the next weather report. Everything was so still. Walter closed his eyes and tried to think of what to do. Suddenly, he heard a little plopping noise on the ground next to him.

He opened his eyes wondering what it could be. Walter looked down and there on the ground next to him was a raindrop.

Walter looked up into the sky, but there were no rain clouds.

"Hello Mr Weatherman," said a little voice.

Walter rubbed his eyes and looked again. A raindrop, when no rain is predicted, and a talking raindrop! Well he was astonished.

He decided to answer the raindrop and so he looked down to where the raindrop was standing.

"Hello little raindrop. What brings you to the park when no rain is on the weather forecast today," said Walter.

"Oh Mr Weatherman, I have been sent down from the rain clouds to see if you can help us fix the weather. All the raindrops are trapped up there in the sky behind those clouds because the wind has decided not to blow. The wind is sulking because he says no one notices him and he can't be seen,' said the little raindrop.

"Oh dear that is terrible. Of course the wind is important and there will not be any sunny and bright weather without the wind to blow away the clouds. What can I do?" asked the Walter the Weatherman.

"Would you talk to the wind, Mr Weatherman?" asked the little raindrop.

The weatherman wondered how he would talk to the wind, but then he smiled because he had just been talking to a raindrop.

Suddenly he heard a whooshing noise in the trees. The tree next to him began to sway and move from side to side. The weatherman looked puzzled because the other trees were not moving. Then he realised this must be the wind!

"Whoo woo," was the next sound the weatherman heard.

He decided to answer.

"Hallooo whoo are youoo," said the weatherman hoping it was the wind. He also hoped that the wind would appreciate the oo sounds from the weatherman.

"I am the wind – woo woo," was the reply.

The weatherman nodded to himself and decided to carry on the conversation.

"Nice to meet you Mr Wind, you do such a lot of hard work for us," said the weatherman.

The wind huffed and puffed as the weatherman tried to talk to him.

"Why have you stopped blowing clouds away Mr Wind?" asked the weatherman.

The wind huffed again and the leaves in the trees blew around the weatherman.

"I am cross," said the wind. "No one notices me, people don't see me. I am invisible. I have decided to just not blow any more," said the wind.

"Oh Mr Wind you _are_ important. The weather needs you everyday. There are so many important things that you do," replied the weatherman.

"Like what," huffed the wind.

The weatherman knew that it was really important to give the wind a boost to his morale and to come up with a whole lot of things that the wind did to help everyone.

"Well Mr Wind, you know without you the leaves won't fall in autumn. Without you children can't fly kites or watch bubbles blow in the air. Mr Wind the clouds need you to blow on them up so the rain drops can collect and fall to the ground and give water to thirsty plants. Mr Wind you are a very important part of our weather," said the weatherman.

"Well Mr Weatherman, I don't feel important. I think you must say some important things about me on the weather channel. If I feel important, I may come back and blow those grey clouds away!" said the wind. Then the leaves on the trees rustled and the wind disappeared.

Walter the Weatherman felt quite exhausted by his conversation with the wind. He noticed his hair was all ruffled and his tie had blown over his shoulder. He straightened himself up and was about to go back to the recording studio when he heard the tiny voice of the raindrop.

"Mr Weatherman, will you help us?" said the little raindrop.

Walter nodded his head and went back inside. He had to come up with a plan to make the wind happy otherwise the weather was not going to work and then what would Walter do. He did not want to speak about grey skies every day.

Walter went home and prepared for the next weather report. He collected a fan from his friend Harold and a kite from his nephew Rupert. Then Walter made a wind sock out of an old handkerchief. That should do it thought Walter. He was going to put on a wind show for the next weather report.

The next day Walter went to his recording studio to talk about the weather. He had decided this show was going to be different. He set up the fan at the side of the studio and then he had his different things to show the audience that the wind was important. He wanted everyone who watched the weather channel to say 'wow' the wind is amazing. Then after the show he was going to tell everyone to go outside and shout out loud – 'wow the wind is really amazing.'

Walter felt very proud of his idea. His wind weather show went off very well. The fan blew like the wind and everything he planned worked perfectly. After the show Walter went back to the park. He was so excited to see that there were people in the park looking up and saying – wow the wind is really amazing. Walter hoped the wind was listening!

Walter sat down on the bench in the park and waited to see what would happen next. He was sure he felt some wind in the trees. The wind grew stronger and Walter noticed leaves blowing across the park. He looked up in the sky and saw some clouds being blown around. They looked like they could be rain clouds. Rain that's just what was needed. No more grey skies, but perhaps some nice big thunder clouds and if the wind blew hard enough maybe the clouds would make some rain fall. Walter remembered his little raindrop friend. He had said all the raindrops were trapped up in a cloud waiting to fall when the wind could blow them to the right place.

Walter looked up again, sure enough there were some big rain clouds. There was some blue sky too and as he watched he was sure the sun was thinking of coming out. Suddenly there was a rumble of thunder and a big drop of rain fell on the path in front of Walter. Then another drop and another. Walter was about to run inside when he heard a familiar voice.

"Thank you Mr Weatherman. You did the trick. The wind was so happy to hear people shout how wonderful he is he stopped sulking and started to blow again," said the little raindrop.

Walter was happy too. He ran inside to take shelter from the rain, but as he looked up he saw a rainbow in the sky. What a wonderful sight! Walter was pleased to see a rainbow with all it's beautiful colors. It was stretched across the sky. Walter knew at that moment he had been a great weatherman.

Chapter 6: The day Johnny went bananas

Johnny was a curious child. He got up to so much mischief.
Johnny's mom remembered the different adventures he had
while he was growing up. The time he fell in a bin of waste
paper and was nearly recycled. The day he rode down the hill
and his brakes failed. He landed up in the duck pond. He sat in
the shallow water and wailed because he had duck weed on his
head. There were never any dull days with Johnny.

One day Johnny had to go to the hospital. He had fallen in the
playground and hurt his little finger. His mom took him to the
reception and he was put in a wheelchair while his mom filled in
all the forms. The doctor came and had a look at Johnny's little
finger and shook his head.

"Now be brave son, we may have to do some x-rays to see what
you have done to your finger," said the doctor.

Johnny wasn't worried about x-rays. He was enjoying all this
extra attention. The doctor left the room and a nurse arrived.
She had some interesting stickers and tags to put on Johnny's
wrist. She looked at Johnny's little finger. It did look a bit odd
and not like his other little finger.

"Ooh what did you do to your little finger?" asked the nurse.
Johnny started to tell the nurse about the game he was playing
in the playground. He was swinging and climbing on the jungle
gym. Johnny and his best friend were pretending to be
monkeys on the jungle gym. They swung from the bars and held

on with one arm just like monkeys do. They chattered like monkeys too and scratched under their arms like monkeys do. All the other children in the play ground laughed at Johnny and his friend Alex.

Suddenly Johnny lost his grip on the monkey bars and fell down onto the ground. He fell in a funny way. No one was laughing as they realised that Johnny had landed on his hand and he was in pain. One of the children quickly ran to call a teacher. Johnny sat there under the monkey bars holding his hand and being very brave. His friend Alex jumped down from the jungle gym and came and sat beside him.

"Are you alright, Johnny?" asked Alex.

Johnny just shook his head. His little finger was very sore.

His teacher arrived with an ice pack for Johnny to hold. He was taken to the office so the school could call his mom.

"What were you doing?" asked the school secretary.

"I was pretending to be a monkey and doing some tricks in the playground," said Johnny.

The secretary shook her head, she knew about Johnny and his tricks. He had been in the office before for other little accidents. She remembered the day he tried to build a beanstalk in the classroom with tables and chairs. It was so the children could experience climbing up to the giant's castle he explained to the teacher when the children came back from their lunch break. Johnny was in trouble that day for being in the classroom when he shouldn't be, and for building a dangerous beanstalk. He had been sent to see the principle.

"Johnny, this is a creative idea, but a very dangerous one," said the principal.

Now Johnny was sitting at the hospital. He liked the kind nurse. She asked Johnny a few questions. She said she was sorry he had to wait. The doctor would be there soon to take the x-rays. It was nearly lunch time. Johnny was going to get a snack. The nurse just wanted to check if Johnny was allergic to anything and asked Johnny if he had any allergies.

Johnny told the nurse he was allergic to bananas. They laughed because Johnny had been pretending to be a monkey and now he was telling the nurse he was allergic to bananas.

"Well I am just going to make a note of this allergy," said the nurse.

 She wrote BANANAS on a tag and put it on Johnny's wrist. He looked at the tag and nodded.

"Bananas," Johnny muttered to himself.

The nurse left the room and said Johnny should just wait quietly for the doctor. Johnny looked around, but before long he was getting restless. He wondered if the wheelchair could move around. Johnny only had one hand that he could use. He released the brake and slowly pushed the one wheel with his good hand. The chair started to move and as Johnny pushed harder the chair moved a little faster. He was moving round the room, but oh dear, he was going round in circles. The wheelchair was only going in one direction because Johnny was pushing with one hand. Round and round he went until he started to feel dizzy.

Johnny stopped the wheelchair and because he was really tired now and feeling dizzy he closed his eyes and went to sleep. While he was sleeping another nurse came into the room. She looked at Johnny asleep in the wheelchair and noticed the tag on his wrist.

BANANAS!

 The nurse shook her head and was very worried about this little boy, who had gone bananas, and was left alone in a wheelchair. The nurse wondered if he should rather be in the children's ward and so she took Johnny to a private room in the children's ward. Johnny was still fast asleep and had no idea that the nurse thought he had gone bananas and that she had taken him to the children's ward and into a private room.

The nurse went off to call a doctor to come and help with this patient.

Now Johnny's mom had finished filing in the forms and went back to the x-ray room to tell Johnny what was happening. She opened the door only to find Johnny had disappeared! Johnny's mom was very upset. Where was Johnny?

Johnny's mom rushed back to the hospital reception to tell them her son had disappeared. She was so worried because she knew Johnny could get up to all sorts of tricks. Now what was she to do? The x-ray doctor came along ready to do the x-rays, but now there was no patient!

The doctor spoke kindly to Johnny's mom and said she shouldn't worry there were cameras in all the rooms. They went together and watched on the camera monitor to find out what had happened to Johnny. Mom and the doctor went to the security office to look at the camera replay of the time Johnny was in the x-ray waiting room.

There, sure enough they saw Johnny sitting in the wheel chair. They saw the nurse talking to Johnny and writing different tags for him. Finally they saw the nurse write BANANAS on the tag and put it on Johnny's wrist. There was no sound to the security camera, mom and the doctor could not hear what the nurse asked Johnny.

"How dare she write that Johnny is BANANAS!"said mom in a cross voice. "He may be very mischievous, but he is certainly not going bananas,"

The doctor tried to calm Johnny's mom down while they could watched the next part on the camera replay. They needed to know where Johnny had gone. The next thing they saw was Johnny going round and round in circles as he steered the wheelchair with one hand.

Mom gasped, it did look as if Johnny had gone bananas. Then Johnny stopped going round in circles and he closed his eyes and fell asleep. Mom was relieved then another nurse came into the room. She looked at the tag on Johnny's arm.

BANANAS.

The nurse shook her head and gently wheeled Johnny out of the x-ray room and down the passage to a private room at the children's ward.

As quickly as they could mom and the doctor ran to the children's ward where Johnny was being kept. They walked into the room and there was Johnny. He was just waking up and smiled as his mom walked into the room. The doctor went over to the wheelchair to look at the tags on Johnny's arm. He saw the one that said BANANAS and then he burst out laughing. Mom looked shocked, but the doctor explained the tag was about allergies and Johnny must have said he was allergic to bananas. Then Mom smiled too and bent down to give Johnny a hug.

"Oh Johnny, we are so glad we have found you," said Mom.

Johnny looked a bit confused. He did not know he was lost and he wondered why he was in another part of the hospital. Mom explained how he had been given a tag that said 'BANANAS' and the nurse though he had gone a bit crazy.

"Now lets get this little monkey x-rayed," said Mom.

Yes and no more monkey tricks," added the doctor.

Chapter 7: Double Vision

The Gregory twins were absolutely identical. If you saw them standing together you felt you may have double vision. It was two of everything. Double trouble their dad used to say. Their parents often struggled to tell them apart, but Mrs Gregory had a special way to know the difference. Grant Gregory had more freckles than his twin brother, Peter Gregory. Everyone else could not tell the difference between the twins. The boys were best friends and did everything together.

One of their favorite things to do was go to the forest near by and climb trees. The twins were very good at climbing trees and could get to the top of the highest trees in the forest. Their mom had told them not to go deep into the forest, but to stay on the edge where they could still see the village and the houses below. They loved to look down on the farm. Farmer Brown had a beautiful farm. When they were up in the tree all the animals looked like toy animals down below.

Peter and Grant set off to climb trees. They promised their mother they would not go anywhere else, except the trees and maybe to the farm. They each had a favorite tree and would race each other to climb up to the top. They kept their word and climbed their trees on the edge of the forest. They took a good look out over the farm land and the pathway that led to another village. The twins climbed their trees and sat back to admire the view. Peter pointed out the horses on the farm and the new foal that was running after its mother.

After a while Grant was so comfortable in his tree, propped up against a branch, that he fell asleep. Peter climbed down and called his twin to come on down because he was going to the farm. Grant did not answer.

"Come on Grant. I am going home and on the way I want to visit Farmer Brown's stable to see the new foal," said Peter.

Grant still didn't answer. That made Peter a bit angry and so he started walking to the farmer's stables thinking Grant would follow him. Grant was still up in the tree and fast asleep. Suddenly it started to rain. A few drops woke Grant up. He sat up and thought he should climb down the tree now. He tried to pull away from the branch he had been resting on when he realised a branch had caught into his shirt and he was stuck. Now here he was right at the top of the tree and he couldn't get down. He heard some footsteps walking along the path and he called out.

"Help, help I am stuck up this tree and its raining," called Grant.

Walking below the tree was Mr Rogers, the builder. He stopped and looked up and saw Grant.

"Hold on there now. I will go and get my ladder at the builder's yard. I will have you down in no time," said Mr Rogers, as he set off to get a ladder.

Mr Rogers had the ladder and was walking back to the forest to rescue Grant. He was muttering under his breath about this poor boy who was stuck in the tree and how he must hurry to get there and rescue him.

Then coming along the path Mr Rogers saw another boy. He looked exactly like the boy in the tree. Mr Rogers stopped right there in his tracks. It was Peter on his way back from visiting Farmer Brown's foal. He stopped to greet Mr Rogers.

"Hello Mr Rogers," said Peter.

Mr Rogers stopped and put down the ladder. He looked sideways at Peter. Then he said:

"What are you doing sending me to collect a ladder when you are not stuck up a tree?" Mr Rogers, was clearly very annoyed that the boy he saw in the tree was not really stuck.

"I am not stuck in a tree Mr Rogers," said Peter.

Mr Rogers looked irritated and huffed as he went back to his builder's yard to return the ladder. Then he carried on back along the path on his way back to the next village. He was just walking under the trees at the edge of the forest when he heard a voice shouting for help again.

"Help, help, I am stuck in this tree," shouted the voice. Mr Rogers looked up and saw the same little face looking at him from the top of the tree. He scratched his head and was very puzzled and then rather irritated.

"OK I will go and get the ladder, but you stay there in that tree until I get back," said Mr Rogers.

"I can't go anywhere a branch is hooked into my shirt," shouted the voice at the top of the tree.

Grant looked down and was puzzled. Why did Mr Rogers tell him he had better stay in the tree. He was stuck there. He couldn't move with this branch caught in the back of his shirt. He was well and truely stuck. Grant was also annoyed because his brother Peter had left him in the tree and was nowhere to be found. This did not seem at all fair.

Mr Rogers went back to the builder's yard and collected the ladder. He hoped that naught boy stayed up in the tree. He had the ladder over his shoulder ready to walk back down the path. Then as he walked round the corner he saw Peter again.

"Where are you going with that ladder?" asked Peter.

Mr Rogers was furious.

"Now look here young man," he said as he put down the ladder.

"I am not going up and down the path with this ladder to get you out of a tree that you are perfectly capable of getting out of yourself!" Mr Rogers scowled at Peter.

"I am sorry, maybe I can help you with the ladder," said Peter.

Now Mr Rogers wondered why Peter wanted to help him with the ladder. He agreed that the boy could help him. Mr Rogers was very suspicious of this boy, who should have been up a tree, wanting to help him. This time he would go along with the boy helping him and then maybe he could understand this silly trick and stop running up and down for a ladder. He would know if this was true or just a false alarm.

"Come on then, pick up the end of the ladder, and lets hop to it," he said.

Mr Rogers and Peter walked back down the road with the ladder. Peter was looking around because he had not seen Grant. He wondered if Grant had decided to go home and not meet him to look at the new foal on farmer Brown's farm. The foal was so cute and Peter was sorry Grant had missed out.

When they reached the tree Peter looked up and saw Grant looking down.

"What are you still doing stuck up there in the tree?" Peter shouted.

Grant looked down and shouted back, "I am stuck here because a branch has hooked into my shirt and I can't get down!"

Then it was Mr Rogers turn to look very surprised.

He looked up at the face peering down from the tree and then he looked at the face standing next to him. He saw the same faces and scratched his head. He thought his eyes were playing tricks on him. He was seeing double.

"Oh my word, there are two boys," he said.

Peter laughed as he realised why Mr Rogers had been so confused. He had muddled up the twins and had thought that Peter was playing a trick on him. The boy in the tree and the boy he met along the road were two different boys. Well not that different because they were twins. Identical twins.

Peter climbed up the tree on the ladder Mr Rogers kindly held for him. Peter helped Grant to unhook the branch from the back of his shirt. The two boys climbed down the tree and stood in front of Mr Rogers.

"My goodness me you two are like peas in a pod," said Mr Rogers.

The boys introduced themselves to Mr Rogers.

"Thank you Mr Rogers for helping to get Grant down from the tree," said Peter.

"Yes Mr Rogers thank you for being so patient and not giving up on me," added Grant knowing how irritating it must have been for Mr Rogers to go back and forwards for the ladder.

"No problem boys I am glad there wasn't something wrong with my eyes!" laughed Mr Rogers.

Mr Rogers thought he was suffering from double vision seeing two boys who looked exactly the same under the tree in the forest.

Double vision laughed the twins, they had been called double trouble, but never double vision.

Chapter 8: Grandma's most unusual knitting pattern

Sally's grandma loved knitting. She knitted for the whole family. Cardigans, beanies, blankets, everything you can imagine. Whenever you saw grandma she was knitting.

"We are off to town Gran," called mom. "Would you like to come along?"

"Yes dear. Just getting my knitting," Gran would say.

"Its time for soccer practise. Wanna come and watch Gran?" Sally's brother Chris would ask.

"Coming now. Just getting my knitting," Gran would call out.

Dad said Gran was attached to her knitting. Gran told dad that it was important to keep busy. Gran had some interesting stories to tell about her knitting. There were many occasions when Gran had come to the rescue with her knitting.

"Hey Gran, the soccer team needs scarves for the championships next week. Can you help?" Chris asked one day.

Gran nodded and went out and bought the wool in the school colors. She made scarves for the whole team. She made coach Roberson a beanie too. That made coach very happy and he bought Gran a box of chocolates. That made Gran happy.

When winter came Gran noticed the sausage dog shivering in the kitchen. She sat down and there and then made Klaus the sausage dog an extra long winter coat. He wore his coat to the park. The coat was admired by everyone at the park. The next day Gran was given orders for dog jackets. She set to work and made lots of jackets. Now every time you go to the park in winter you see dogs running around in gran's jackets.

"You are a trend setter Alice," said her friend Mavis.

Gran just smiled, she loved being appreciated for her knitting.

One summer holiday the family went to the beach. Everyone was sure Gran would not be knitting on her holiday. Well they were wrong. Gran had her knitting basket and needles on the beach. Mom and dad could not help laughing. They thought the basket was a picnic basket. No such luck, Gran was ready to knit! What pattern was she choosing this time?

"Bikinis," said mom with a gasp. "You are knitting bikinis!"

Gran nodded and began to knit bikinis! She knitted away and took her bikinis to the gift shop on the promenade. The bikinis were for little girls and they just loved them. When Gran grew tired of bikinis she made sun hats and the girls loved those too. Everyday there was a new bikini on the beach. All the little girls came out wearing bikinis and had matching sun hats. When Gran left the beach she promised the gift shop she would continue to send bikinis for the little girls to wear.

What would gran's knitting lead to next? Everyone could see gran was tired of knitting blankets and scarves. She needed a new project. Winter was coming, but everyone had plenty of jerseys, beanies, bed socks and hot water bottle covers. Gran was sitting in the kitchen watching mom make some coffee.

"Oh no, the coffee gets cold so quickly in the winter," said mom as she heated her coffee up again.

Suddenly, mom heard the clattering of needles behind her and in a few minutes there was a mug warmer. It was just the right size to fit round mom's mug of coffee.

"Thank you mom, what a great idea," said mom to her mom.

Well, that was the worst thing to say to Gran, the knitting machine. Out came stacks of scraps of wool. Gran created the most amazing mug warmers. They were made in lovely warm winter colors. Some had flower patterns or fair isle patterns. Stripes or just plain. Gran could knit them all. Once our house had enough mug warmers Gran moved on to the coffee shop down the road and made mug warmers for them. When other coffee shops saw the mug warmers they ordered mug warmers too. That was gran's very busy winter project. Millions of mug warmers.

Everyone in our town knew gran and her knitting. Gran even made it on the news once. She caught a thief with her knitting. Gran was sitting at the supermarket. She had finished her shopping and was waiting for mom to finish hers. Then they would go home together. Gran was waiting by the check out. She had her knitting of course. She was knitting some fancy tie backs for the curtains. Gran had made up a pattern to knit the tie back and then turn it into some kind of loop that would hook round the curtains.

Gran had an amazing way of being able to knit without looking. She had those needles clattering away row by row, but at the same time, her keen eyes were looking around the room. She could hold a conversation with you and meet you eye to eye. She never dropped a stitch. Gran had complete control over those needles and before you could say 'Baa baa black sheep,' she had knitted up all the wool.

Now back to the story of gran and the supermarket thief. Gran was sitting quietly by the checkout waiting for mom. Everyone was busy with their groceries. Gran was knitting, but her eyes were looking around and she saw a stranger walking around the shop. He did not really look as if he was buying anything. He looked suspicious. He did not have a trolley. Gran decided to pretend she was knitting, but her eyes were watching this stranger. She saw he had a bag round his shoulder and he was shop lifting. The man was loading his bag with chocolates and sweets. Gran kept her eyes on the man. He walked out of the shop. He thought he was going to get away with the loot he had in his bag.

Well, as the man got close to Gran she waited and watched. Gran had her curtain tie backs ready. When the man was in easy reach Gran swung those tie backs out like a lasso artist. The tie backs whipped round and caught the thief around his ankles! With an almighty crash he tripped and fell down on the floor in front of Gran. Gran stood up and pointed one of her knitting needles in the man's back.

"You are under arrest. I am holding you at needle point," said Gran in a gruff voice.

The man was so shocked he just lay on the ground shivering. All the things he had stolen were thrown across the floor. The thief had been caught in the act.

Gran stood there triumphantly while the police came and arrested the man. They picked him up and put on handcuffs. The man was shocked to see he had been caught by an old lady with a knitting needle. Gran's picture appeared in the paper and that made her famous around the town.

Gran had some stories to tell about her knitting and the different patterns she had made. She was never short of ideas or interesting projects. Gran loved telling her stories to her friend Mavis in the park. Mavis laughed and laughed about gran's stories, but the funniest story of all was the one gran told about the missing wool. Gran had been knitting in the park one day and she had been chatting away with Mavis. Gran had not really been paying attention to her knitting, because when Gran and Mavis got together there was more chattering and nattering than clattering of knitting needles. Finally it was time for Gran and Mavis to think about going home. Gran looked down to find that her ball of wool had fallen under the bench.

"Oh Mavis dear," said gran. "Have you seen my ball of wool?"

Mavis looked around, but she could not see the wool. Then the two friends noticed a trail of wool leading away from the bench and across the grass in the park. The original ball was looking very small under the bench. A long trail of wool led awayto under the bushes.

"Someone has had the cheek to take my wool," said Gran.

"Let's follow the trail and see who has taken your wool," said Mavis.

The two ladies picked up the ball of wool that was left and began winding it up as they followed it towards the bushes. There was a rustle in the bushes and Gran and Mavis wondered what they would see. They were so surprised. There at the end of the wool was a little mouse. A little mother mouse who had decided the wool was a perfect lining for her nest.

Gran and Mavis stopped and stared. A mouse using gran's knitting wool to make a nest. It was time for the two ladies to tiptoe away. Gran cut the wool so the mouse could have it all.

"I wonder what stitch the mouse is knitting?" said Mavis.

"I think it's moss stitch," said gran and she laughed about that very unusual knitting pattern.

Chapter 9: An Afternoon with an Alien

Alan's mum was getting very tired of asking Alan to finish his lunch.

"Stop playing with your food Alan," she said.

Alan was pretending his banana was a rocket ship. He held it up over his head and then swooped it down over his plate of food. The he began twirling his saucer and making strange noises. Sort of whirring noises! His mum wondered what he was imagining now. A flying saucer, alien space ship of some kind. Round and round it spun on the table while Alan made some swooshing noises.

Eventually his mom was so angry she banged on the table and told Alan she was leaving the room.

"Alan, you must finish your lunch and get on with your homework. When I come back I want to see a clean plate," said Alan's mom in her most cross voice.

Alan hardly looked up, he was so involved in his flying saucer story. He gave the saucer a few more twirls and behind him he heard the door to the dining room slam. Mom had left.

Alan was sure his saucer could be a flying saucer if he made it whirl fast enough. He made it spin round and round. The saucer was going faster and faster. It made Alan feel dizzy and then it spun out of control off the table. It seemed as if the saucer was flying round the room. Alan rubbed his eyes and blinked.

The saucer *was* flying round the room. Alan ducked as it flew over his head.

"Steady," said Alan as the flying saucer came closer. This time Alan ducked under the table and tried to hide. The saucer was out of control.

What a shock Alan got when he came face to face with something, or was it some one, under the table. The creature nodded and looked at Alan. Then Alan heard a thump and the flying saucer landed on the carpet behind him.

"Beep, shoop, sneep," said the creature while it pointed to a dial on its chest.

Alan looked at the dial and read what it said 'Choose your language' followed by some names of different languages. Slowly and carefully Alan twisted the dial to English. The little creature nodded its head.

"Hey, good to meet you, my name is Altairion. What is your name?" asked the creature in perfect English.

Alan stared in disbelief. Who was this creature and what was he doing under the table? How did it get there, was that a saucer on the carpet? Alan was sure this was an alien. He hoped it was a friendly one.

"My name is Alan, nice to meet you too. What are you doing under my table?" asked Alan.

Alan was polite to the creature. It did look like an alien with three eyes and several legs. Alan didn't want to stare.

Somehow the alien had taken control of Alan's saucer. Alan waited for the alien to reply. It was difficult to focus on the alien because of its multiple eyes and arms. The alien toddled around under the table scooping up crumbs like a vacuum cleaner.

"My mom would like you," said Alan trying to make some small conversation with the alien.

He could see the alien was useful as it sucked up the crumbs under the table. One of the alien's arms had a vacuum nozzle on the end. Alan was fascinated as the alien destroyed all the crumbs under the table. When everything was cleaned up the alien hopped up onto the table. His vacuum nozzle went straight to the plate of lunch Alan had not eaten. Alan watched in disbelief as the alien sucked up his lunch.

"What are you doing with my lunch?" asked Alan.

"Recycling. You don't want to eat this lunch," answered the alien.

Then he proceeded to suck up all the lunch from Alan's plate. When all the food had disappeared the alien hopped on down to the flying saucer and attached the nozzle into the side of the saucer. Alan heard a humming noise and realised that all his lunch had been turned into fuel for the flying saucer.

"We don't waste anything on our planet. I am so glad I landed here where I could find fuel for the flying saucer," said Altairion.

Alan took another look at the saucer lying on the carpet. The saucer had grown and was humming like a top. The alien jumped towards the refuelled flying saucer. He looked around with his three googly eyes and beckoned to Alan.

"Would you like to come for a spin?" asked the Alien.

Alan could not believe what he was hearing. An alien asking him to go for a ride in a flying saucer! That was unbelievable. Alan nodded and walked towards the saucer on the carpet. He was not sure how he was going to get in. As he got nearer to the saucer a sliding door opened and Alan stepped right in. He did not have to think twice.

"Welcome aboard my flying saucer, space ship," said the alien.

Alan gasped. This was a dream come true. He was on a flying saucer and an alien had asked him to go for a ride. The alien showed Alan to a seat in front of the controls. Little lights flashed all over the place. The alien sat next to Alan and showed him how to put on his seat belt. Then as if by magic the flying saucer started to take off.

"Where are we going?" asked Alan.

"We are going to take a flip around my planet. Well its actually a star. The supernova star called Nouvella. It is a beautiful star and I am sure you will enjoy the ride," said the alien.

Alan was so excited. He sat glued to his seat as he felt the flying saucer spin and take off. It flew out of the window and up into the sky. It flew so fast that Alan hardly had time to blink. Right infront of him the alien was pointing out other stars in the sky. Alan watched everything he had learned about in science fly past. The Moon, Mars, Jupiter, and Saturn. What a treat. The flying saucer flew on.

"Look over there," said the alien and he pointed to something huge on the saucer screen.

Alan looked and coming towards them was a huge ball of fire. It glowed red and orange in the sky. There were hundreds of shining lights all around the big ball and every so often a spark like a firework would fly off into the atmosphere.

"We are going to hit the sun," said Alan in a panic.

"No Alan, not the sun, that is a supernova star. Novella, my star and my home," said the alien.

Alan did not look quite sure about that and wondered what the alien had in mind as they grew closer to Nouvella. The alien hovered for a while so that Alan could catch his breath. He explained the star did look like the sun, but it was really a star. Nouvella was surrounded by luminous dust that made it look so bright.

"We won't be landing today. I just wanted to take a spin in space with you," explained the alien.

Alan nodded. He was quite glad they would not be landing. This had been a huge experience without landing on the planet as well. Suddenly he felt some butterflies in his stomach. He realised they were descending, going back to earth.

"Nearly home," explained Altarion, the alien.

There was a final drop and Alan felt himself going through the window and landing next to the dining room table. What an experience. A trip to the stars with an alien. Alan was still rubbing his eyes in disbelief. The alien came and thanked him for allowing him to refuel and he was about to go on his way. Alan smiled as he looked across the table and noticed his lunch plate was wiped clean.

"Oh thank you Altarion," said Alan. He was grateful that he didn't have to eat his lunch.

Alan waved good bye to the alien and looked back at the table again. He suddenly remembered he had homework to do. It was a crossword about space and planets. Alan filled in the clues in no time. All the names were fresh in his mind after his afternoon ride through space. He just put his pencil down when mom came into the room.

Alan could see she was ready to have a battle, close to World War 3, with her son. Alan was sitting at the table with a clean plate in front of himself and a crossword puzzle completed for homework.

"Alan, how did you manage all that so fast?" asked mom.

Alan smiled. He knew how easy it had been to do everything super fast. An afternoon with an alien had sorted everything out nicely.

Chapter 10: Beyond the Clouds

Justine and Helen loved lying on the grass and looking up at the clouds in the sky. They imagined all kinds of fantastical cloud creatures. Unicorns and flying horses were their favorites.

"How wonderful it would be if we could get up there into the clouds and meet the fantastic animals we have imagined," said Justine.

"We could have quite an adventure. Do you think unicorns and flying horses really exist?" asked Helen.

The girls continued to stare up into the sky as the clouds rolled by. Then they noticed some very dark clouds building up. A storm was brewing. Justine and Helen picked up their things ready to go inside. Suddenly there was a mighty flash of lightening and a huge crash of thunder. They were startled and dazzled by the light from the lightening. A different sort of light shone around them. There in front of them was a unicorn. It looked just like the unicorn in the clouds.

The unicorn bowed gracefully and stepped back as another flash of light appeared, followed by the sound of wind. It was a flying horse who landed next to the unicorn. Then the thunder started again and this startled the magical creatures.

"We will not harm you," said Helen gently.

"No you are safe with us," added Justine.

The unicorn nodded and took a few steps forward. The flying horse tucked its wings away and followed closely behind the unicorn.

"We need your help. Will you come with us?" asked the unicorn.

The girls looked at each other and nodded. Helen climbed onto the back of the unicorn and Justine sat on the back of the flying horse. Then the girls felt themselves being lifted up into the sky. Up towards the clouds. The white, fluffy clouds that they looked at so often. They were above and flying beyond the clouds. Everything looked white and fluffy around them.

The unicorn and the flying horse slowed down to a stop and let the girls off to stand in the clouds. It was like standing in moving snow. A really strange sensation. A rumbling in the distance reminded them that they were here to help with a problem. Something to do with the black cloud in the distance.

The unicorn and the flying horse came forward to introduce themselves.

"I am Esmerelda," said the unicorn.

"I am Mariah," said the flying horse.

The girls introduced themselves too and followed the two mystical creatures towards a beautiful, white castle. It was still so different for them to walk in the clouds. How often had they thought of doing just that. Justine could not resist kicking up some cloud dust. She watched it puff up into the air and fall down gently.

"Girls. We do need your help. There is a storm coming and we need to find shelter before...." but Esmerelda's words disappeared into the clouds.

"Yes, we must hurry," said Mariah.

The girls followed the unicorn and the flying horse into the white castle. It seemed to appear in the clouds as if by magic as they grew closer. The front doors of the castle opened by themselves and everyone walked into a magnificent hall. Out of nowhere two thrones appeared and the girls sat down.

The doors of the castle closed. The sound of thunder echoed outside and the windows grew dark. The black cloud seemed to close in on everyone. Then Justine and Helen noticed other magical creatures come into the room and gather behind the unicorn and the flying horse. All sorts of white animals. An Arctic fox and a white rabbit followed by a group of white mice. All creatures they had seen in the clouds so many times.

"You must be wondering why we have brought you here," said Esmerelda.

"Yes, we are wondering what could be the problem," said Helen.

Esmerelda bowed her head and began to explain. She told the girls that life up here above and beyond the clouds was filled with peace. Everyone lived their lives in harmony and there was very little disturbance. It was a floating kind of existence as they drifted across the sky. Making interesting shapes was the way of life here. Now there was a disturbance, a terrible noise, that was getting worse.

Mariah looked out the window where the black clouds were gathering. All the little cloud creatures followed her gaze and shivered.

"Does this have something to do with the black cloud?" asked Justine.

Mariah nodded. "It is the thunder dragon. He is angry about something, but we don't know what it is. He sent us a letter and no one here can read it. Do you think you girls could help us?"

Esmerelda went to fetch the letter and handed it to Helen.

Helen opened the letter and began to read what it said. Then she smiled.

"What are you smiling about?" asked Esmerelda.

Helen passed the letter to Justine and Justine smiled too.

"Oh dear. You all have nothing to fear," said Justine.

The letter was an invitation. The poor Thunder Dragon had been trying to invite everyone to a party. He wanted to celebrate his birthday, but every time he opened his mouth to invite the other cloud creatures his voice boomed out and scared everyone away. He tried to creep closer, but when he got near everyone ran away because they feared his darkness.

"Dear friends, I have tried to lighten up the sky with some lightening bolts, but that seems to scare you all even more. I really would like to celebrate my birthday with you and I promise I don't want to scare anyone," wrote the Thunder Dragon in his letter.

Everyone looked around the room. Esmerelda stepped forward.

"If only we had known that the Thunder Dragon was not feeling fierce and wanting to send darkness over our beautiful land," sighed Esmerelda.

"Thank you for reading the letter to us," added Miriah.

Now everyone had to decide how they were going to reply to the invitation. Who was going to be brave enough to go and answer the Thunder Dragon. The cloud creatures started to discuss how they would reply. Even though the Thunder Dragon had promised he was not wanting to hurt anyone the cloud creatures were still afraid.

"We need a volunteer," said Esmerelda. "Who will go and face the dragon?"

Helen and Justine looked at each other and nodded. They said they would go on one condition.

The cloud animals looked worried, but nodded in agreement. Justine wanted the animals to follow behind her and stay at a distance. In this way they would show the Thunder dragon they were going to come to his party. Everyone nodded and followed the girls out of the castle door.

Justine and Helen led the way. They looked behind them to see if the other cloud creatures were following them. They saw a cloud of creatures piling up behind them. Like a huge mountain of white shapes. The animals all grouped together to show the Thunder Dragon they were ready to enjoy his party.

At that exact moment there was a mighty flash of lightening and a crash of thunder. It shook the cloud floor and everyone quivered. Justine and Helen stood firm and waited for the Thunder Dragon to appear. Slowly and carefully the black Thunder Dragon appeared out of his dark cloud. He bowed his head as a sign of peace. He did not throw any lightening bolts around.

"Friends," said the Thunder Dragon and everyone felt a small rumble as he spoke.

"Friends among the clouds. I would like to invite you to my thunder party. Please say you will come," the Thunder Dragon said as he leaned forward.

At that moment the cloud creatures pulled closer together and their cloud gathering grew bigger and taller. Some creatures hiding behind the others and some standing on top of others. There was a mighty tall tower of cloud shapes and sizes.

Esmerelda stepped forward. She looked brave and beautiful. The unicorn bowed to the dragon and told him everyone would be there even though they looked a little shy right now. Then she turned to Justine and Helen. She thanked the girls for their help and said that it was time to return them to earth. The girls climbed on the magical flying animals. Soon they found themselves safely back in their garden. They looked up at the sky as Esmerelda and Miriah flew off back to the clouds.

"Look at those clouds," exclaimed Justine.

Way up in the sky the clouds had piled up into a great, puffy mountain.

Their mom came out to call the girls inside for tea.

"Look at those cumulus clouds. We may get a storm later," she said.

Justine and Helen smiled. They knew why the cumulus clouds gathered high up in the sky. It was time for a celebration with the Thunder Dragon and the cloud creatures.

Chapter 11: The Mysterious Tunnel

Mandy and her brother Mark were staying with their uncle for the holidays. They were sad that this was going to be their last holiday with Uncle Fed. They had so many wonderful holidays staying at his mansion. High on the hill it overlooked the sea and they loved going there exploring the old house and playing in the garden.

"This will probably be your last holiday here with me," said Uncle Fred sadly.

Uncle Fred explained the house needed a lot of work and he did not have the finances to do the repairs. He had decided to sell. There was a buyer coming to make the last arrangements. Uncle Fred was very busy sorting out papers and working out details for finally handing over the house.

"Run and play children and don't get up to mischief," said Uncle Fred.

Mandy and Mark walked out into the garden. They wished they could help Uncle Fred. They walked to the bottom of the garden where the old tool shed was. A dusty old shed overgrown with ivy.

"I have an idea," said Mark. "Lets see if we can clear out the old shed and turn it into our secret hideout while we are here."

"That's a good idea, it will give us something to do," added Mandy.

The two children set to work getting the shed cleaned up. It was really a mess. Uncle Fred kept all his new garden equipment closer to the house now. Ride on mowers and leaf blowers were the modern gardener's tools. Mark and Mandy saw old rakes and shovels hanging in the shed. They found an old couch and a dusty table. They cleaned them up and put them neatly in the room. The old garden shed was starting to look quite homely.

"Wow! We have spent a whole day here," said Mark.

"Let's pack a picnic for tomorrow. I am sure Uncle Fred will be pleased to have us out of his way again," Mandy said excitedly.

The next day Uncle Fred was delighted that the children had found something to do. He told them the old shed had not been used for years. Uncle Fred had often told the children stories of the grand house long ago. It had been in the family for many years. There had always been an Uncle Fred. Every first born boy was called Frederick William Robert Barnesly. Mark was very relieved when his mother did not continue the tradition.

Mark and Mandy went off happily to the shed with a picnic basket. They had decided to give it a good sweep today. Uncle Fred had given them some cushions to put on the couch. The shed was going to look really cosy. The children rolled up the carpet and pulled it out from the shed. They both began to sneeze. What a lot of dust and some sea sand. That was strange, sea sand in the gardener's shed! The sea was far away over the cliffs. The could hear the sound of the waves and see the ocean stretching out in front of them. There was a steep path down to the beach on the other side of the garden. It was a long walk only for the most energetic! When everyone wanted to go to the beach they would get in the car and drive down to the little beach village.

The children dragged the carpet outside and while Mandy swept it with a stiff garden broom Mark went back inside to sweep the floor. He was just moving the couch when he noticed something interesting.

"Mandy, come quickly!" shouted Mark.

Mandy dropped her broom and rushed inside to see what Mark was getting so excited about.

She looked at the floor where he was pointing and gasped. There was a trap door. It had been covered by the couch and the old carpet. What was a trapdoor doing in the old shed?

"Shall we try to open it?" asked Mark.

"Lets just have a peep. It is probably just old tools or maybe somewhere to store coal for the old kitchen stove," said Mandy.

It was quite a strain to open the old trapdoor. The children had to scrape away dust and dirt that had been there for years. The catch was rusty and once again there was sea sand. How peculiar, sea sand in a shed far away from the beach.

Finally with a loud creaking noise the trap door started to open. A musty smell came up from the space under the trapdoor. The children wondered what they would find. They peered into the dark, but could see nothing.

"I think we need to come back tomorrow with a torch," said Mark.

Mandy nodded. It was getting late and they could not see anything under the trap door. It would be better to be safe and return with a torch. The children packed up their picnic and felt very excited about exploring the next day. They decided not to tell Uncle Fred until they knew more about what secret lay under the trap door.

The next day Mandy and Mark turned to the garden shed. They had found an old torch and some rope that Mark thought might be useful. They dressed in track suits and wore their beanies and hiking boots.

"We look like explorers," said Mark.

Mandy smiled. She could see Mark was enjoying this little adventure. When they got to the shed they pulled away the carpet and opened the trapdoor. Mark switched on the torch. There in front of them was a winding, old staircase. It was cut out of the rock. Once again the children noticed sea sand.

"This is a tunnel of some sort," said Mark.

" I wonder where it goes?" asked Mandy as she watched Mark shine the torch down the steps. The tunnel stretched in front of them, but they could not see the end of it.

"Shall we explore further?" asked Mandy.

"Yes, let's go down this tunnel and see where it goes," said Mark.

The children decided to tie the rope to the trap door. It would help if they needed to follow it back up to the shed. Then with a quick high five they set off down the tunnel. It twisted and turned as it followed the rocks. At one point the children stopped where a side clearing had been carved out of the rock.

"Hush! Listen to that noise," said Mandy.

They stopped and listened. It was the sound of the sea. Waves crashing on rocks and wind blowing. The tunnel led down to the sea. Now the children understood why there had been sea sand in the tool shed. Someone had been using this secret tunnel to get down to the beach. They carried on down a few more steps to get to the bottom of the tunnel and into a large cave.

"Wow," they gasped together. The tunnel led to a cave on the beach. The children walked carefully towards the opening of the cave. It was a very small opening, hidden behind some rocks. When the tide was up the opening would be hidden completely. The back of the cave was higher than the front and joined to the tunnel.

"No one has been here for years. Look at these old barrels at the back of the cave," said Mark as he ran around exploring everywhere. He called Mandy over to look at an interesting sea chest. It was almost covered in sand, but made out of wood and very strong.

"I wonder what is in here?" said Mark who was always very curious.

A few crabs scuttled out from under the chest and gave Mandy a fright. She was keen to get back to the shed now. Mark insisted on taking a closer look. He pulled and pushed on the lock of the sea chest and managed to get it open. He lifted the lid and wow what a sight he saw!

"Mandy, come and see this. I think we have the answer to all Uncle Fred's problems," said Mark.

Mandy walked over slowly to avoid any more crabs. She gasped too. There in the chest were gold coins and treasure, pirates treasure! Mark and Mandy remembered Uncle Fred telling them about the pirates who used to hide treasure round here. No one had been able to claim the ancient fortunes that were thought to be hidden in caves under the cliffs.

"Oh Mark, we have found the pirates treasure. Uncle Fred will be able to use the money to save the house and we will have our holidays here again.

The two children were so excited about what they had found. They jumped for joy and with a gold coin in their pockets, to show Uncle Fred, they ran back up the tunnel and to the house.

Their holiday was going to end happily ever after, there was no doubt about that.

Chapter 12: Grandpa's Magic Motor bike

My grandpa's name is Harley. Harley Davis, and you guessed it, he loves motor bikes. Grandpa had so many stories to tell of his motor bike days and how he rode around the country with his Harley friends. Mum and Dad used to nod and smile about his stories, as if they really didn't believe him. I believed him and I loved grandpa's Harley Davidson stories.

One day Grandpa called me down to his old shed at the bottom of the garden. He dusted a few cobwebs off the door and put a rusty old key into the lock. He twisted the key and the door creaked open. What I saw in the old shed that day had my heart beating. I looked up at grandpa with a huge smile on my face!

Gramps, as we all called my grandfather, walked to the back of the shed where there was something covered with an old sheet. He lifted the sheet and said:

"Tah dah," like a grand opening of a circus act. Gramps revealed a beautiful shining Harley Davidson motorbike. This was no dusty old relic. It was gleaming from top to toe.

"Gramps," I gasped. "Where did you get this amazing motorbike?"

Gramps just smiled and beckoned me to come closer. He was so proud of his motor bike. The thing that interested me, as I got closer to the bike, was that everything in the old shed was dusty and dull. The motorbike was shining and smart. No dust on this old bike. Then I wondered how the bike could look so shiny and new.

"Come here, Hairy legs," said Gramps using the nick name he had given me since I was a toddler.

I went across to look at the bike and listen to what Gramps was going to tell me. I knew it was going to be interesting.

"This here bike is a magic machine," said Gramps in a whispering voice.

I nodded as I was sure Gramps loved his bike so much he would always call it a magic machine. I watched Gramps stroke the bike lovingly and then gently move it to the side and take the rest of the old sheet off the back.

"Wow, that's a beauty Gramps!" I exclaimed.

Gramps burst with pride and then he began to explain that the bike was *really* magical. He told me he would come down to the shed in the middle of the night and go for a spin. Sometimes he went round the neighbourhood. Sometimes he rode on the beach or up and down mountains.

"I go anywhere I want, Hairy legs!" said Gramps in an excited voice.

I began to wonder if Gramps was getting a bit forgetful and having dreams about the bike. Then I wondered why it was in such top mint condition. Gramps put the sheet back over the bike and leaned towards me.

"Ya don't believe me do ya?" said Gramps with a twinkle in his eye.

I looked sideways at Gramps and didn't want to spoil the chance of listening to any more of his motorbike stories. I just nodded and pretended to be interested. Gramps put his arm round my shoulder and we walked out of the shed.

"Meet me here tonight at midnight and I will show you a thing or two," said Gramps as he winked his eye and gave me a nod.

I went back home and couldn't wait for midnight. Finally the kitchen clock struck twelve. I counted twelve bonging sounds and there it was, midnight. I hopped out of bed and went downstairs to find the front door open. Down at the bottom of the garden I could see a faint light on at the shed. Gramps had already made his way to our meeting point.

I walked slowly and carefully to the chosen meeting point. My heart beat a bit faster as I grew closer to the door and heard the gentle hum of a motorbike starting up. There was gramps sitting astride the bike. He had his Harley helmet on and his black leather jacket. The one I had seen behind the door in his bedroom. Gramps was ready to ride!

"Hey Hairy legs, glad you could make it," said Gramps.

I walked over slowly to the bike, the magic machine that Gramps had spoken so lovingly about. He revved the bike gently and handed me another helmet. Then Gramps beckoned me to jump up on the bike. Once I was sitting comfortably he turned the bike to face out of the door.

"Ready?" he asked as he turned to look at me.

I was ready, but ready for what? Slowly Gramps edged towards the door. Then as he reached the open door of the shed he put the bike into a full throttle. We leaped forward and straight up into the air. I gasped and held onto Gramps. He let out a mighty laugh like a roar and he put his head down. The bike was airborne and Gramps held it steady as we rose up into the sky!

We were flying. This really was a magic machine.

"Where to Hairy legs?" Gramps called over his shoulder.

I was so blown away by the fact that we were flying I could hardly get enough breath to speak. Then I remembered I had always wanted to see the Grand Canyon.

"Grand Canyon, Gramps!" I yelled at the top of my voice.

"Gottcha," said Gramps and he turned the bike in the direction of the Grand Canyon.

What a magic ride. We were on our way to see one of the wonders of the World. When we were nearly there Gramps pointed out some of the landmarks. We rose up high above the canyon and followed the route of the Colorado River. We felt like eagles riding on a thermal as we looked down into the canyon way below. Gramps was in control of this magical ride.

 At last he said it was time to go home. He turned the magic motorbike towards home and before he could say 'Hairy legs' we were cruising back into the garden shed. I was feeling dizzy with the excitement and the speed of the ride. Gramps took it all in his stride. He set about cleaning the bike and putting the dusty old sheet over it. He did not want mom or dad to discover his secret.

In the morning at breakfast mom complained of the noises she heard in the night.

"Did you hear some funny noises last night?" asked Mom.

Gramps and I looked at each other wondering if mom knew about the motorbike. Gramps had been hiding the bike for a while in the shed. Mom was sure Gramps was up to something, but she was not sure what he was plotting and planning. She had spoken kindly and gently about Gramps when he came to live with us. Mom explained that Gramps had a very interesting imagination. She did not look surprised when Grams looked up and answered her question.

"No, no funny noises," said Gramps. "Except for the flying motorbike that rode off to the Grand Canyon. Did you hear that one?" asked Gramps.

I just held my breath. Why was Gramps telling mom about the motorbike in the shed. He was going to give away his secret and that would be the end of any more adventures.

Mom looked up and tutted across the table. She shook her head as she always did when Gramps told his stories. It was his over active imagination again.

"Now we all know about your stories. You went to the moon the other day and what about the time you took a ride to the Arctic and back. Here we go with another one. Really Gramps, you are filling young heads with fanciful ideas. What will you come up with next?" said my mom with a sigh.

Gramps looked at me across the table and gave me a wink. I shook my head because unless it was a dream that we both had last night I was sure Gramps and I went to the Grand Canyon on a magic motorbike.

After breakfast Gramps looked at me and pointed to the shed. We went down to check on the motorbike. It was still there. Gramps took out his world atlas and we had a good look for our next destination. It was so hard to make a decision. So many places to go and so many wonderful things to see. We could go anywhere on Gramps' magic motorbike. We decided to point a finger at the map and go where our finger pointed. Gramps let me go first.

I closed my eyes and Gramps opened the map. He counted to three. I put my finger on a place in the world. I opened my eyes and Gramps and I looked very excited about the next destination. We were going to Africa!

Chapter 13: Message in a bottle

Summer holidays on the beach were always a favorite for the Murray family. They went to the same beach every year as their family holiday. They knew the rock pools and the tides like they knew the palm of their hands. Mom and dad were happy to relax in the sun while Gus and Tanya explored the beach. It was always a very happy holiday time.

"Let's run down to the rocks and see what we can find," said Tanya.

The two children ran down to the rock pools. The tide was going out and so they could paddle around and watch crabs and little fish flitting around. The rock pools were always interesting, but Gus and Tanya had noticed this holiday that the beach was not as clean as it used to be. They saw empty plastic packets washed up on the shore among the driftwood and broken shells.

"This makes me sad," said Tanya as she picked up a plastic bag. On their way home the children collected a few other bags and put them in the dustbin. The children felt disappointed that people were not being kind to the beach.

"I wish we could think of a way to clear the beach of all the litter," said Gus.

Tanya nodded in agreement. That night Tanya had a dream about pirates arriving on the beach and forcing anyone who threw litter around to walk the plank. She saw a pirate ship in her dreams called 'The Jolly Junk Bin.' It was a giant dustbin that floated on the sea and came in to the beach to collect all the litter. The pirate ship collected litters as well.

In the morning Tanya told Gus about her dream. He laughed and said what a pity they couldn't use some pirate tactics to sort out all the people who threw litter onto the beach. The two children enjoyed Tanya's dream so much they decided to play a game called pirates and plastic! The searched the beach for litter and threw it in the bins provided.

"Well done you two," said the life guard as they walked past.

"Wish we could get more people interested in picking up litter," said Gus.

The life guard nodded. He was sad too about all the rubbish that littered the beach. It was a real problem. Gus and Tanya picked up more litter and then they went back to their beach cottage.

When they were having supper their mom asked what they were doing on the beach today. The children told her they were playing a game of pirates and plastic. Mom was very interested.

"How do you play pirates and plastic?" she asked.

"Oh, it is just an imaginary game that we thought of after Tanya had a dream about pirates coming to the beach to sort out the litter problem. We just made up the game to help us enjoy picking up litter," said Gus.

Mom nodded her head and commended the children on their efforts to keep the beach clean. She told the children how important it was to have people like themselves who loved a clean litter free beach.

"What will you be up to tomorrow?" asked mom.

"I guess we will be on pirate patrol again," answered Tanya.

"Well look out for a message in a bottle. Maybe there is a shipwreck out there with survivors to rescue," said mom, as she winked at dad.

The children went to bed laughing. They were not sure if they would ever find a message in a bottle, but they were sure there would be more litter to pick up the next day. It was Gus who had a dream that night. He dreamed about a shipwreck and because mom had mentioned a message in a bottle Gus dreamed of messages in bottles. Not just one bottle, but hundreds of bottles came floating across the waves. Gus had watched them from his look out place in his dream. They looked like the nasty floating bluebottles that came to the beach sometimes.

"Breakfast," called mom to the children.

Mom wanted to know if there had been any other weird dreams. Gus told her about the messages in bottles. Mom laughed as she remembered the conversation last night.

"Well, I wonder if you will find a message in a bottle today," said mom.

"A message in a bottle will just look like litter!" exclaimed Gus.

"Well, we are picking up litter, lets just check all the bottles we see in case there is one with a message," said Tanya.

Gus laughed as they played their pirate game. He thought he saw Tanya our of the corner of his eye looking in rock pools and along the shore for a message in a bottle. There were many bottles but none of them had a message. Then Tanya picked up one she thought had a message. She shrieked with delight and turned the bottle upside down. Then she shrieked with fright because a crab just jumped right out of the bottle. It landed on Tanya's feet and scuttled off into the waves.

"Ha, ha that was a weird message," laughed Gus.

"Not what I was expecting," said Tanya and she laughed too.

On the way home Gus talked about how the crab got into the bottle and what fun it was to watch Tanya's face when he jumped out of the bottle. When mom saw them she laughed at the crab in the bottle story. Then mom had an idea.

"Why don't you children try and put a message in a bottle and see who gets it. It could be something about the litter problem," said mom.

"That's a good idea," Gus said enthusiastically.

"We could say something like 'pick up litter or else!" shouted Tanya in her most cross voice.

"Well, that would be a bit unfair because someone picking up the bottle is probably trying to help," said mom

The children nodded in agreement, but they liked the idea of a message bottle. They thought and thought about what they could do that would be different. Mom came up with another clever idea.

"Why don't you put a message in the bottle to say something about a prize will be awarded! A prize for everyone who finds a bottle with a message in and collects a bag of rubbish," said mom.

Gus and Tanya looked at each other and then they began to laugh. It was such a good idea. They could put ten message bottles out there and ten people would collect ten bags of rubbish. It was an ingenious idea.

The next day the children had ten bottles ready with ten messages. Each bottle had a bag with it rolled up in the bottle ready to collect the rubbish. The collection point was at the life guard.

"We need a reward I think," said Tanya.

"What could that be?" asked Gus.

Mom had *another* idea. She said she would see if she could get tickets to the beach concert donated as prizes for whoever took the message in the bottle seriously. Gus and Tanya were so excited about that idea. Mom had some connections to the entertainers. A cousin of hers was in the band. She was sure he would give them some free tickets for such a worthwhile project.

The children were so excited about their clean up plan. They rushed down to the beach and carefully put the ten litter pick up bottles around in different places. Then they sat back to see who would pick up a bottle and show some care for their beach.

They didn't have to wait long. Two boys came along with their dog. The little dog sniffed out the bottle and ran up the beach to show it to the boys. They were about to throw the bottle for their dog to chase when they noticed something in the bottle. They unscrewed the lid and took out the message and the litter bag. Gus and Tanya could see the excitement on their faces as they ran up and-down the beach collecting litter. Then the boys ran to the life guard to show off their bag of litter and collect their prize. Two tickets to the beach concert.

That day the children had a wonderful time watching different people pick up the bottle and look curiously at the contents. Then they would run around collecting their litter. Some people kicked the bottle further down the sand and did not bother to pick it up. They were the losers, no free tickets for them.

The children were delighted when all the bottles had been opened and bags of litter had been collected. Mom had managed to get free tickets for Gus and Tanya too. It was a great end to their holiday. But best of all was the message in a bottle that had help clear some litter from their special beach.

Chapter 14: Ronnie and the Marathon run

Ronnie had been a talented runner since the day he could put his feet on the ground and could walk. Actually Ronnie never really walked, he just stood up and ran. His parents were amazed. They thought their toddler should slow down a bit. There was no slowing Ronnie down he was built to run.

When Johnny started school his teachers were impressed with this little boy who just ran everywhere. There was no stopping Johnny. When his grade one teacher, Mrs Solomon, wanted to send a message to the school office she always sent Johnny. She knew that her message would be delivered 'super fast.' Johnny won all the grade one races at the sports day. He even won the junior trophy for the best little runner.

Johnny's mom and dad realised Johnny had talent as a runner. Johnny's dad encouraged him to practise his running and together they would go to the park and jog round the field. At first Johnny's dad could keep up with Johnny. Then Johnny started overtaking his dad and out running him everyday. Dad had to sit on a bench and huff and puff while Johnny sprinted round the field.

That's when dad decided he would sit and take Johnny's times and help him beat his record when they went for training. Johnny's school noticed how determined Johnny was to succeed as a runner. They put him in the long distance marathon team as soon as he was old enough.

Johnny just loved running and although he worked hard at school his running was the most important thing in his life. One day, after training, a very important man come up to Johnny.

"Hello Johnny. I have been watching you run and I see you have talent and determination," said the man as he put out his hand to give Johnny a handshake.

"Thank you," said Johnny as he looked at the man curiously.

The man handed Johnny a card with his name on it. Mr Grant Simpson. Director of Keen Sports. Mr Simpson was a talent scout for this well known sport's company.

"I would like to offer you a sports bursary," said Mr Simpson.

Johnny's eyes just lit up. He knew it was getting difficult for his dad to afford expensive running shoes and track suits. Johnny took the card and ran home to show his dad.

"A man at sport's practice gave this to me and said he could give me a sports bursary," said Johnny.

Johnny's dad took the card and congratulated Johnny. He said he would call the director, Mr Simpson, that very morning. Johnny was so exited and couldn't wait to tell his friends

Everyone at school was interested in Johnny's running. His teacher did remind Johnny that school work was important too.

"No good in just being a runner now Johnny," she said.

Johnny nodded he wanted to make time for everything including his friends. Johnny's best friend Richard was a good runner.

Not as good as Johnny, but pretty fast. Richard ran in the running team with Johnny.

Johnny and Richard loved running cross-country runs together. They always kept up with each other and enjoyed the rough and tough route that their coach chose. Johnny and Richard used to tell jokes on the way. It kept them laughing as they ran through the mud puddles and crossed rough roads together.

"Knock knock" said Richard.

"Whose there?" answered Johnny.

"Eye sore," said Richard.

"Eyesore who," asked Johnny. He was ready for a silly answer.

"Eye sore from all this running," answered Richard. The two boys laughed and laughed as they ran over the muddy puddles.

Then it was Johnny's turn to tell a joke.

"This is a good one. What do you call a person who runs behind a car?" asked Johnny.

"Silly?" answered Richard.

"No, exhaust-ed," replied Johnny. The boys held their stomachs as they laughed and laughed.

The jokes always stopped when they came in sight of the finishing line. This was Johnny's time to shine.

Johnny always came in first, except once when he tripped and twisted his ankle. Richard sat with him until help came and Johnny was taken home. Richard did not finish the race that day. He went home with Johnny to give him support and tell a few more of their silly jokes.

"Hey Johnny, this is a good one in case you forget how to run again," said Richard with a laugh.

The joke was something about what do runners do when they forget something.

"What do runners do when they forget something?" asked Richard.

"Jog their memory," laughed Johnny. He had heard that one before.

Johnny's sponsor, Mr Simpson, came to see Johnny and was pleased that he would be up and running again soon. The doctor said Johnny had done well.

"There is a long distance marathon in two weeks time," said Mr Simpson. "And Keen Sports would like you to wear a sponsored T-shirt for the event and Keen Sports track shoes."

Johnny's eyes sparkled. He would be ready. Mr Simpson left and handed over a T-shirt and a new pair of track shoes to Johnny. Johnny's dad was so proud and he suggested Johnny should wear the shoes right away to break them in.

"You can't wear brand new shoes on the day son," said dad.

Johnny knew his dad was right. He started wearing the new shoes immediately. In two weeks time he would be running in a long distance marathon. Richard came round and the two boys started to practice their running to build up Johnny's strength. In two weeks he was ready for the marathon.

The big day arrived. No jokes from Richard on that day. This was a serious race and Johnny needed to impress the sponsors. They expected him to come first and run out in the lead wearing the Keen Sports t-shirt and track shoes. He knew Mr Simpson would be at the finishing line ready to welcome Johnny for the Keen Sport's team. It was going to be a grand finish.

The competitors lined up and Johnny kept pace with Richard at the front of the pack. Johnny knew how to keep back the best in himself for the sprint at the end. He would be bursting out into the stadium in style to show how Keen Sports helped young people to be winners. That was what the sponsorship was all about. Showing how the Sports sponsors helped young people become winners.

Johnny and Richard were doing well. They kept up their steady pace and were ready for the last part of the marathon. Suddenly Richard slipped and fell. This time it was Richard's ankle that had twisted on a rock. Johnny stopped to hold him up.

"Go on Johnny, don't stop for me," said Richard.

Other runners started to pass Richard and Johnny, but Johnny refused to run ahead.

"No Richard you are my friend and you stopped to help me once. Now it is my turn to help you," said Johnny in a most determined voice.

Richard realised there was no point in arguing. He allowed Johnny to pick him up and help him to hobble along the road. They could hear the crowds cheering as the runners came in. Mr Simpson was standing eagerly waiting at the finish line. He had his camera ready to take a magic picture of his winning runner. At first Mr Simpson looked annoyed that Johnny was not there right in the front. Then he began to look anxious as there was still no sign of Johnny.

"I wonder where my lad has got to?" said Mr Simpson.

Then the crowd began to cheer again. They cheered even louder than before. Mr Simpson looked up to see what the cheering was all about. He gasped when he saw his champion runner coming in the final group of the race. Why were people cheering the last runners to come in. Then Mr Simpson saw the reason. There at the back of the race was Johnny. But Johnny was not alone. He was helping his injured friend Richard to the finish line. Mr Simpson was so pleased to see Johnny that he took a picture of Johnny and Richard crossing the line together. Johnny went to apologise to Mr Simpson and expected to be in trouble for not coming first.

Mr Simpson was grinning from ear to ear.

"Oh don't worry Johnny, that was awesome! I have a brilliant picture to use for our next promotion." said Mr Simpson. Johnny looked rather confused.

The next day Johnny saw the headlines in the paper with a picture of himself with Richard.

'First or last in the race Keen Sports always make you a winner!"

"You see," said Mr Simpson. "Selling good sports kit is not only about winning.

 He shook Johnny's hand and thanked him for doing his best as a runner and as a best friend.

Chapter 15: Simon the boy who loved Science

Simon loved science. It was his favorite lesson of the day. He couldn't wait to get to the laboratory and dress up in the white science coats and look like a real scientist. The kids in his class thought he was a bit studious and wondered why he loved science so much.

"Are you going to be a nutty professor?" they used to tease Simon.

Simon just shook his head because he did not think science was nutty at all. He enjoyed seeing how chemicals mixed together and made different interesting things. Simon had always been interested in mixing things together. His mom thought he might be a chef one day. He loved being in the kitchen. She watched him mix bicarb and flour and water and other funny things together to make them fizz. Then mom realised Simon was not really interested in baking, he wanted to see what happened when different ingredients were mixed together.

Simon used to listen to the other children tell stories about their adventures and their exciting holidays. Sadly Simon did not have great adventures to talk about. He wished he had a way of showing the other children at school how science was just as exciting as any other activity.

"Science is all about adventures," Simon told his mom one day.

Mom just nodded in agreement because she did not really understand what Simon was talking about. Mom was worried about her saucepan in the kitchen. She had burnt the popcorn the other day and now it was getting hard to get the burnt pieces off the bottom.

"Don't worry mom. there's a scientific answer for that," said Simon.

Simon mixed some bicarbonate of soda and some vinegar together. It fizzed a bit and then it settled in the pot. Mom stood and watched in amazement as the pot was easy to clean after that. Simon stood back and his chest burst with pride.

"You see mom, science even helps in the kitchen," said Simon.

Simon loved science so much he would always volunteer to stay behind and tidy up after the science lesson. The other children would leave happily knowing Simon was there to pack away everything. The science teacher, Mr Edwards, trusted Simon to put everything away and lock up the science room.

"Put the key back in the staffroom, please Simon," he would say after the lesson.

Simon was so happy to do that. It meant he had some extra time alone in the science room. He liked to walk around in his lab coat and pretend to be a nuclear scientist or a medical researcher.

He had collected everything and was busy putting the science lab coats away. Suddenly, he heard a strange noise. A scratching noise and it seemed to be coming from behind the cupboard. He tried to listen more carefully, but it was getting dark and he had to return the key to the staff room.

"I wonder what that could be?" said Simon to himself.

Simon went home wondering about the noise in the science room. The science room was part of the old school and was one of the oldest buildings. Simon's school had a long history behind it. The school even had a museum with some artefacts and treasures from the past.

Simon thought about mentioning the funny noises to his mom, but then he was sure she was not really interested in silly noises in the science lab. Simon carried on thinking about them for a while. He went to bed that night wondering if he should say something about the noises. He decided it would be better not to say anything until he had proof that there was something strange going on.

The next day the children at school found out someone had been into the school museum. Mr Edwards was in charge of the museum, it was part of the science rooms. He had a key to the museum. Mr Edwards could not understand how someone had found their way into the museum when the door was locked. It was a mystery.

Simon wondered if there was a connection between the noises he heard and the missing artefact from the museum. What was missing he wondered. Then the bell rang for school to start. Simon stopped wondering and joined his class for lessons. He checked the timetable and noticed there was a science lesson at the end of the day. That was something to look forward to.

When the end of the day came Simone was the first in line to get to the science room. Mr Edwards told the class how disappointed he was that there had been a mysterious break in. A valuable part of the school's history had been stolen. A beautiful jade stone. It had been found when the original school was built. The children wanted to know more about this stone, but Mr Edwards did not know much more. He said it was jade and must have belonged to something, like a treasure box or a bracelet.

The science lesson began and everyone was interested in this lesson. How to make stink bombs. There was lots of giggling about stink bombs and Mr Edwards made everyone promise they would not let stink bombs free in the classroom. The children agreed stink bombs were for outside tricks. It was a fun lesson and Simon was happy to clear up at the end. He put his stink bomb in a safe place while he gathered all the science lab coats together and put them away.

When he got to the cupboard he heard the strange noises again. Scratching and scuffling sounds. Simon stood in front of the cupboard, he noticed a hole in the back of it. He decided to peep in. He pressed his eye close to the hole and looked carefully through the opening. At first he couldn't see clearly, then slowly a dark shape came into view. Then another dark shape. Simon took his head away from the hole in the cupboard and tried to work out what he had seen.

Simon squinted into the hole again. He saw two men dressed in black and they had a bag with them. They had masks on so he could not see their faces. They looked as if they were up to no good. Simon noticed they were in a basement place that must have been part of the old museum. There was a trap door leading into the museum and behind the intruders was a door leading outside.   Simon was not sure what to do, but he knew science would have a solution. He decided to go home and make a plan to go into action the next day. On his way home he walked round the back of the science lab and the museum. He found what he was looking for, another door. It was hidden behind some ivy, but it was a door. It was nearly covered in the creeper. Simon noticed, as he walked by, that some of the branches had been broken. He nodded to himself, now he was sure someone was up to no good.

Simon could not wait to get to school the next day. He had a plan to catch the thieves. He went to Mr Edwards in the morning to talk to him. Mr Edwards nodded as he heard the plan. Another item had been stolen during the night. It was important to catch the thieves before they raided the entire museum. School went in as usual. At the end of the day Simon went to the lab and Mr Edwards contacted the police for their help outside the old door behind the museum.

Simon put on a white lab coat in case someone was watching and wondering why he was in the lab. Safely in his pocket he had not one, but two of the stink bombs made during the last science lesson. Simon waited until he heard scuffling noises and then he was ready for action. He crept up to the hole in the cupboard and pushed the stink bombs through the hole. Then he covered the hole with a piece of card and stood still to listen.

Suddenly Simon heard coughing and spluttering. He heard footsteps and a door banging. Then the big, booming voices of the police officers.

"You are under arrest," came the official command.

Simon quickly ran out of the science lab and round to the back door where he saw Mr Edwards and the policemen arresting two thieves. The thieves were dressed in black and looked very sorry for themselves. Mr Edwards came to Simon and thanked him for his clever plan.

The next day there were pictures in the paper. Simon, the scientist, was a hero. He had rescued the missing jade stone. The children in Simon's class were impressed with his bravery. Everyone had more respect for science and Simon the Scientist.

Chapter 16: Dad favorite party tricks

My dad just loves playing tricks on everyone and telling jokes at parties. He usually has everyone in stitches at his party jokes. Whenever we have a theme party dad likes to get dressed up and join in the fun.

When I had my eighth birthday dad came dressed as a pirate. He fixed up a real wooden leg and was so convincing the children thought her really had one peg leg. Dad hobbled around the room and kept saying 'aargh' and 'shiver me timbers.'

We did not need an entertainer at the pirate party. Dad was there with jokes to tell and had everyone laughing at his funny comical lines and impersonations of a pirate.

"Why don't pirates take a shower before they walk the plank?" asked dad.

"That's because they will wash up on the sea shore," dad answered his own joke.

Dad had another joke.

"What did the ocean say to the pirate?" asked dad."

"Nothing!" was the answer. "It just waved!"

And just to finish off the joke session dad pointed to his fake wooden leg and said,

"What did I pay for this peg leg and this hook?"

The answer to this joke always made everyone laugh. It was 'an arm and a leg." Many of the children didn't quite get that one, but the adults used to laugh a lot.

My sister had a witch and wizard party and dad decided to be the magician. He dressed up and made a grand entrance with a cape and a magician's hat. He asked all the children if they knew what witches used to race on.

"Vroom sticks," said dad with a great big laugh.

Then he wanted to know what a witches' favorite lesson at school was? Everyone got that 'spelling,' they shouted.

After the jokes and the birthday cake, with trick candles of course, the ones that don't blow out, everyone settled down for dad's magic show. He was already dressed for the part of the magician and had his table of tricks all set up and ready to entertain the willing audience. Dad impressed the children with his find the card trick. We knew the secret behind the trick, but the other children did not guess how dad had arranged the cards. He agreed to show us one year after we pestered him. It was not difficult once you knew the trick.

Dad didn't keep his jokes to birthday parties he was always playing tricks on everyone. My dad's favorite day of the year was the 1st of April, April fool's day. He could go around tricking everyone and yelling April Fool all day long.

Halloween was another favorite of dad's. He was the parent that dressed up to welcome trick or treaters at the front door. He always wore his Dracula teeth and goofy eyeballs to look the part of some Halloween creature. He would ask the children who came to the door if they would like some I- scream cake. When they said yes dad would hand them an empty bowl and then he would scream. When they looked puzzled he would say:

"You wanted I - scream cake! There you have it. I just screamed for you. Do you want some more?" said dad.

The children shook their heads and ran off. Those that stayed on the front door step were rewarded with a bowl of real ice cream. Dad always thought that was hilarious.

Dad never missed an event to tell jokes and have everyone laughing. Christmas was another favorite opportunity. Dad loved to dress up in his Santa suit. On Christmas eve the family would sit round the Christmas tree and dad, dressed as Santa would tell some Christmas jokes.

"Why is Santa good at karate?" asked dad.

"Because he has a black belt!" everyone would shout out. That was an obvious one.

"OK, try this one," said dad with a smile, he never gave up on his jokes.

"What do hip hop artists do on Christmas eve?" asked dad looking pleased with himself. Everyone shook their heads.

"They unwrap!" said dad laughing so much he nearly fell off his chair.

"I think it is time for us to unwrap a present," said mum patiently.

"OK, last joke. What do Santa's helpers learn at school?" asked dad as he looked around the room. Everyone shook their heads.

"The elf-abet," said dad as he clapped his hands together to applaud the joke. Once we had all laughed a bit we were given a present to open. Just one because the rest of the presents, and some more Santa jokes, were scheduled for the next day, Christmas Day.

Last month was mom's birthday. Dad asked her what she would like. Mom thought long and hard and eventually she said she would like a little diamond perhaps. Dad had been promising mom a shiny diamond for years. Dad said he would try his best. Mom thought this year he was going to be lucky.

We should have guessed it would be a trick! What did dad give mom for her birthday? He gave her a pack of cards and a message to say there were lots of diamonds in the pack, but mom was always the queen of diamonds. Then there was a separate box with a present and the queen of diamonds on the top. We were all glad dad had not taken his trick too far. Luckily mom knew dad and his tricks of old.

"When we got engaged, your dad popped a ring in a glass of champagne. Suddenly he realised that I was about to drink the champagne and the ring. He grabbed the glass out of my hand and the champagne spilt all over the table. The ring fell onto my side plate! Then your dad proposed. It was very dramatic!" said mom.

Well as the year went by the time got closer to dad's birthday. Mom and I agreed it was time dad got some of his own medicine. What could we do? We thought and thought. Magic tricks would be no fun. Dad knew them all. Jokes, well he had told all the jokes we could think of. What could we do? Then mom remembered dad was keen on technology. We decided to trick him with the promise of the latest I-pad.

When dad's birthday arrived we were ready. We were going to have a birthday quiz. Dad would have to answer questions to get his birthday present. The trick was to choose several things starting with i. Technical things and then let dad see if he could guess his gift. Mom had managed to organise a special deal through her phone to get dad and i pad. The i pad was tucked away. Neatly wrapped up in a box was another gift. The trick gift.

This was the plan. Dad would have to guess his gift and we all knew he would not get the trick answer because his gift was not really any sort of modern technology. It was electrical, but not dad's kind of technology. We all giggled as we thought of dad getting caught by a trick at his birthday.

On the morning of dad's birthday he came to the breakfast table all cheerful and ready for his present. He had been dropping hints for a few weeks and so he was convinced that he would be getting what he wished for. Usually mom put the birthday gift on dad's place at the table, but this year she did not put a gift there. The gift was hidden behind a cushion on the chair.

Dad came bouncing down to the table all set to unwrap his present and entertain us with a joke or two. He looked surprised when there was no gift at his place on the table. Now it was mom's turn to tell a joke.

"Happy birthday dear. Have you heard the latest birthday joke?"

Dad shook his head not quite sure of what to say. Mom continued.

"It goes like this:

Forget about the past, you can't change it.

Forget about the future, you can't predict it.

Forget about the present, we didn't get you one!"

Dad looked astonished. What, no present? Then mom said dad could have his present if he could guess what it was. Dad smiled a bit then and began to guess.

"An i phone?"

No everyone said together as we were all enjoying the trick.

"An i pad?"

There was so much tension mom decided to put the gift, the trick gift, on the table. Dad began to smile. He took the paper off and opened the box and then he began to laugh. He took the gift out of the box.

"An i-ron!" oh what a clever trick all of you. I guess I have been given a taste of my own medicine," said dad!

Yes, laughter is the best medicine,"added Mom as she handed dad his real present.

Chapter 17: Mission Submersible

Oscar and his father loved exploring the secrets of the ocean. When Oscar was growing up his father took him snorkelling in the rock pools and along the shallow reefs at the sea. When Oscar grew older his dad taught him how to deep sea dive and together they would explore deep water of the ocean.

It was not surprising that Oscar had a real connection to the sea and sea animals. He remembered from a young boy how he had felt an octopus sucking on his leg. When he got a fright and screamed his mom had come running down to the rock pools to see what he was screaming about.

"Ooh, it tickles," said Oscar.

Mom laughed when she realised that Oscar was not in any danger. He was enjoying connecting with the octopus.

Oscar had many happy memories of the sea and his beach holidays. When he was old enough his father taught him how to ride on a submersible exploration vehicle. It was such an adventure. Oscar and his dad could go right under the water. Holding onto the submersible they could ride around like real fish. They wore oxygen tanks and masks to protect their faces. There was nothing nicer than feeling as if you were swimming with a shoal of fish.

Oscar never felt afraid because of his deep love of the sea. Sometimes there were moments when really big fish swam by and Oscar would look around for his dad. If his dad gave him a thumbs up Oscar knew they were fine and he carried on swimming holding his submersible. It was like a mini submarine, but Oscar was on the outside and able to explore around rocks and even dive into sea caves and swim around shipwrecks.

One day Oscar was diving along around some rocks and looking at interesting fish. He loved the brightly colored clown fish. Oscar watched different fish swimming in and out of the rocks. Then he saw something large and mysterious between the rocks where he was planning to swim. There was something really strange about this creature. Was it a monster of the deep?

Oscar decided to swim over to where he saw his dad and get his attention. He was not sure what this creature was. Oscar's dad never let him swim alone and Oscar was really grateful. He wanted his dad to see what he thought about the strange creature hiding in among the rocks. Oscar swam over to his dad and waved and pointed to the surface. Together they floated up to the open water.

Oscar told his dad about the strange creature he saw hidden in the rocks.

"What does it look like, does it have sharp teeth?" asked his dad.

Oscar tried to describe the monster. He told his dad it had very rough skin and looked as if it had made a large nest down under the rocks. Oscar's dad looked puzzled.

"I think we should go and take a closer look. We may need a deep sea torch and an under water camera to take some pictures," said Oscar's dad.

They decided to go back to their beach cottage and get the things they would need. Then they took their boat out to where the creature was.

When they were ready they tipped their submersibles into the ocean. Oscar led the way. Cautiously they reached the place where he had seen the strange creature in its nest. Oscar watched his dad move slowly and careful towards the creature and take some pictures. They saw some movement but could not make out what was in the nest. It was very well camoflaged in different shades of brown like shadows.

Oscar's dad indicated they should go to the surface and look at the pictures on the digital camera. They floated up and returned to the waiting boat. Oscar's dad took out the camera and they both had a look.

"It is not a nest!" exclaimed Oscar as he looked closely at the photograph.

No, it was not a nest. It was a tangle of netting pulled into the rocks and caught there. The terrifying thing was not a monster. It was some creature trapped in a tangle of netting and pulled under the rocks. Oscar and his dad could not make out what creature it was, but they knew they must go back down to the tangled mess and try and rescue the creature, the monster in the deep.

Oscar's dad collected some tools from the boat. A sharp knife and some cutting tools. Together Oscar and his dad went back to the place where the monster and its nest were hidden. They were careful not to make any sudden movements and anchored their submersibles away from the nest. When Oscar and his dad got close to the nest they realised it was not a nest after all. It was a tangled mess of a fishing net. It was a terrible knotted jumble of mesh wrapped around something. They could not quite see what it was. As they got closer the creature began to snap at them. It was very afraid.

Oscar's dad cut gently at the fishing net and then they could see a clearer picture of the creature. It had a beak like mouth and two eyes covered with heavy eyelids. The creature had a leathery back and flippers. Oscar and his dad nodded to each other they knew what the creature was. It was a sea turtle. They did not have to be afraid of a sea turtle even though it was very big. The poor turtle had its flippers caught in the net. Oscar's dad swam closer to try and cut away more of the net. He did not want the turtle to twist and become more tangled. He needed to work fast because although a turtle can stay underwater for a long time it still needs to get to the surface to breathe.

Finally the giant sea turtle was free and it began to wiggle and move out of the trap it was in. It swam very fast and Oscar and his dad tried to keep up with the turtle. The sea turtle looked back towards the two divers. They were holding their submersible diver vehicles and trying to swim with the turtle. It looked as if the turtle was waiting for them. They caught up to this beautiful sea creature and they had a swim through the waves together. It was as if the turtle was saying thank you. Oscar noticed a piece of the net was caught around the turtle's neck. It looked like a tag as it floated in the water. Oscar and his dad could not get near enough to remove it. The turtle did not seem to mind.

That evening Oscar and his dad went down to sit on the sand dunes and watch the tide come in. Suddenly they saw something really amazing. It was time for turtles to come up onto the beach and lay their eggs. Several leatherback turtles were making their way up the beach to dig their nests and lay their eggs. One turtle stood out from the rest. A beautiful leatherback with a tag around its neck. It was the very turtle that Oscar and his dad had rescued. She was coming to lay her eggs with the rest of the turtles.

Oscar and his dad watched the turtle climb up the beach and make her nest. They saw how she dug with her strong front flippers and then scrapped back the sand with her back flippers. When the eggs had been laid the turtle covered them and patted them down. Then she flipped sand this way and that to make it look as if nothing had been buried there.

"Wow. That is amazing dad," said Oscar.

"Yes it is. We saved more than one turtle today," said Oscar's dad.

That is not the end of this wonderful story. Oscar became a marine biologist and followed his dream to study sea turtles. He learnt so many interesting things about these amazing creatures. They can sense when seasons change through a pink spot on their heads. It tells them when the sunlight changes. Every year a sea turtle returns to the same beach where it lays its eggs. Oscar went back to the beach he had sat on as a young boy. Every year his turtle, the one he and his dad had rescued, would come onto the beach. It was her 'birth beach.' Oscar named her Clara, meaning light. He knew it was Clara because she had the same tag round her neck. In the light of the moon Oscar would watch the giant leatherback, Clara, lay her eggs. He was sure when she returned to the sea each year she gave him a nod as if to say, thank you, here's another batch of sea turtle eggs. Another mission submersible completed.

Chapter 18: The Runaway Kite

Kei had a new kite. He was given a beautiful, dragon kite for his birthday. Kei could not wait to fly his kite. He played with it in the garden and listened to the rustle of its colorful tail. He didn't want the kite to really fly yet. Kei was waiting for the weekend when his dad had promised to take him to the park.

When the weekend came Kei and his dad went out to the park with the kite. Dad was going to show Kei how to let out the string of the kite and slowly with little tugs and runs into the wind he would get the kite to rise up into the sky. Kei was so excited. He knew this kite was special and it was. The kite seemed to have a mind of its own. Kei's dad stepped out of the car and started to walk towards the park the kite was already pulling at its strings. The kite was twisting and turning before Kei even got to the open field.

"Hey dad this kite really wants to go," said Kei to his dad.

Kei's dad just smiled. He was eager to get the new kite launched on its first flight.

Kei held the kite and his dad started to run back then when he could feel the kite tugging to get away he called to Kei to let go. Whoosh, the kite flew up into the air. A few tugs from dad on the string and the dragon kite was going higher and higher into the sky. Dad was holding on and gently pulling the kite to keep in control.

"Can I have a go now dad?" asked Kei.

"Sure son, it is your kite," said dad.

Kei's dad was ready to hand over the string when a sudden gust of wind caught the kite and lifted it higher into the air. Kei was not strong enough to hold on and the string pulled out of his hands. The kite swooped down at that moment and Kei reached forward to try and catch it, but he tripped on the root of a tree. Kei's dad continued the chase. He wanted to catch the kite but the kite was on its way into the next field.

"Come quick lets hurry to the car and drive to the next field. Perhaps we can catch up with the kite," said Kei's dad.

Kei and his dad rushed to the car and drove to the next field. They could still see the kite and wondered if they could catch its tail. The kite dipped and swayed across the field. Suddenly it swooped down towards Kei and his dad. The kite flew past. Kei thought he saw the kite wink one of its bright dragon eyes. He did not have time to be sure before the kite, the runaway, kite flew away and disappeared.

Kei was very disappointed. He felt as if the kite had wanted to get away. This was the first day of trying to fly his beautiful dragon kite and it had flown away. Kei and his dad drove home slowly and they looked everywhere for the kite. Kei thought he saw the flick of a colorful tail over the fields but he could not be sure.

Now the kite had flown off on its own journey. It had wanted to be free for a long time. Cramped up in a box the kite was eager to get away and fly. When Kei took it out and the kite saw the world outside the box it was even more eager to get going. The kite had waited for the right moment to wriggle free and go. The kite felt its string loosen and then suddenly the kite caught a gust of wind and off it flew.

The kite wiggled its tail and fluttered in the wind. It looked down at the field below and saw Kei and his dad standing at the edge of the field. The kite smiled. It was free. The kite flew off and passed over trees and grassy fields. It was flying over a small part of the forest when it heard a soft crying sound. The kite was not sure what the sound was all about but it was not a happy sound.

The kite decided to try and see where the sad sound was coming from. It wiggled its way down towards the trees. It didn't want to get too close because of getting its tail stuck in the trees. Then the tree saw what was making the sad sound. A kitten, a little grey kitten was stuck in the branches. Immediately the kite fluttered down to where the kitten was stuck in the tree. The kite dangled its tail close to the kitten.

The kitten looked up and started to try and catch the tail of the kite. The kite wiggled its tail a bit more and the kitten patted the air a bit more. Then the kitten realised what the kite was trying to do. The kitten jumped up and caught the kite with two paws and it tuck its claws into the tail of the kite. The runaway kite lifted up in the next breath of wind and carried the kitten out of the tree and into the grass below.

The kitten was so happy. It jumped and twisted in the air to say thank you to the kite. The kite was so pleased to have helped and it flew up into the sky again. The kite was having a wonderful time and off it flew to see what else it could do. The kite wondered if there were other rescue missions that it could be part of.

Sure enough it wasn't long before the kite spotted a nest floating down a stream. There were two baby birds in the nest. They were chirping at the tops of their voices. Their nest must have fallen out of the tree on the river bank and here they were sailing down the river but not able to steer their boat or swim to safety. The kite was ready to rescue and flew over the little birds in their nest. Once again the kite dipped and took a dive down towards the birds in their nest. The kite managed to get the bird's attention with his colorful tail. One of the birds caught the string of the kite in its mouth and then the kite flew across the river to drag the boat to the other side. The little birds cheeped and chirped all the way. The kite did not mind it just carried on flying and pulling the little baby birds to safely.

The kite felt so pleased with itself. It had achieved two rescue missions since finding its freedom. The kite thought it had found its calling in life. A rescue kite. Not a runaway kite but a rescue kite. The kite flew up into the air again. It was very pleased with being able to fly around and do whatever it liked.

The kite was flying over some houses in a small town. It looked down and saw a small boy sitting in his back garden. The boy looked sad. He was crying and the boy's father was trying to tell him everything would be OK. The kite flew down to get a better look. As it flew closer to the boy the wind grew stronger and the kite was pulled towards the roof of a house. The kite felt its tail get caught on something on the roof. A spiky piece of metal sticking up by the chimney. The kite did not know this was Kei's house and his tail was caught in Kei's TV aerial.

Kei and his dad went inside and sat down to watch their favorite TV show. They were just getting comfortable when the TV went a fuzzy. The picture looked strange. Dad stood up and tried to fix the picture but there was not changing the fuzzy look. Dad was a bit irritated and decided to go outside and see if there was something wrong with the aerial. Kei's dad stood on a rock in the garden but he couldn't see anything so he went to the garage to get a ladder.

Kei's dad set the ladder up against the roof and climbed up to see if there was anything making the TV aerial go funny. Imagine his surprise when he saw Kei's kite tangled in the aerial. The kite's tail was firmly wrapped round the aerial. Kei's dad had a chuckle to himself. He carefully unwrapped the kite and then went into the house to show Kei what was causing the trouble.

Kei was so happy to see the kite again and the kite was really happy to see Kei. Its runaway days were over. The kite was happy to be Kei's kite and stay at home.

Chapter 19: The most unusual rescue story

Ben was very adventurous. He never missed an opportunity to try something daring. Ben loved all kinds of outdoor activities. He liked climbing, hiking, swimming and exploring. Ben was always looking out for the next adventure.

Ben and his father used to hike and climb mountains together. They really enjoyed exploring caves too. Ben's dad had taught Ben how to wear a head light and have his food in a back pack so his hands were free to hold rocks and climb. They would pack a picnic together. Mom would wave goodbye as they set off for the day. Rusty, their Jack Russell terrier, would get very excited when he saw the back packs come out. He knew that Dad and Ben were off on a hiking adventure.

When Ben grew older his dad stopped coming on the hiking trails. Ben's dad had found a new hobby. He was part of a carrier pigeon organisation. He and his friend had set up a carrier pigeon place behind the house. Dad spent a great deal of time learning about the pigeons and their amazing ability to find their way home.

Ben's dad entered competitions. He loved taking his pigeons off to a field where a competition was being held and then releasing all the pigeons to fly back home. He knew they would always come back. Ben helped sometimes, but really in his heart he knew he wanted to be out hiking and finding caves.

One Saturday dad said he was going to enter a competition.

"Would you like to come along Ben?" dad asked.

Ben shook his head. He wanted to walk to the caves in the hills. They were not too far away and mum had said she would pack a picnic for him. Rusty was very excited because he knew Ben would take him along. In the morning Ben took his picnic to fit in his back pack and a few treats fro Rusty. Dad was out at the back sorting out the pigeons. He was meeting his pigeon friends for lunch and then they were going to release the pigeons to fly home.

Mom waved goodbye. She was happy to be having a morning to herself. Ben and Rusty enjoyed walking up the rocks and along the path that led to the caves. The caves were very unusual caves. Parts of the caves were open and looked out to the sky. These openings were called skylights. If you went inside the caves you could walk and crawl along passages to reach some of the skylights. Hikers were warned to be careful of the skylights and the passages. Ben was a good hiker and knew his way around the rocky hills. He reached the highest point of the climb and sat on a rock to eat his picnic. Rusty was scratching around and exploring the rocks. Ben was about to pack up and find his way back when he heard a rustling of wings. He looked up into the sky and saw the pigeons. He nodded to himself. Dad and his friends must have released the pigeons. They were on their way back to their nesting place at home.

Ben shielded his eyes and looked up into the sky. He stood up to get a better look and at that moment he lost his balance. Suddenly Ben was slipping down the gap between the rocks where he had been sitting. Ben tried to hold onto some grass and some bushes. Ben was slipping and falling into a crack between the rocks. Ben could see the light, but he could not get out of this opening between the rocks. Ben had fallen into a skylight opening.

He called out, but there was no one to hear him. He heard Rusty sniffing around. Ben was not injured, but he could not pull himself out of the gap in the rocks. He called for Rusty. Rusty tried to reach Ben, but he couldn't get down the steep slope to the crack in the rocks. Rusty seemed to sense that Ben was in danger and he ran off.

What was Ben to do now. How would he tell his mom and dad where he was. He hoped Rusty would come back with help, but what if Rusty couldn't find his way back. Mom and dad would be getting worried. Then Ben heard a strange noise. It was a flapping noise. Ben wondered if it was a bat. Bats live in caves. Perhaps he had disturbed a bat when he fell through this crack. Ben looked up and there sitting on the branch was a bird. It was not any bird, it was one of his dad's pigeons. It was sitting there looking down at Ben. Ben did not want to scare the pigeon so he just cooed gently.

The pigeon cocked its head to the side as if it was listening to Ben. Ben put out his hand gently and cooed some more. The pigeon hopped down towards Ben. The pigeon seemed to know Ben and that he was in trouble. Ben began to think about what he could do to get the pigeon to help him. Then he remembered the pigeon was a carrier pigeon and if Ben tied something to its foot the pigeon would carry on home and take something to his dad.

Ben lifted the pigeon gently into the cave where he was and he held the pigeon in one hand just the way his dad had shown him. Then Ben took a piece of thread off the track suit he was wearing and tied it round the pigeon's foot. Ben stretched his hand up as far as he could and stuck it out through the skylight. Then he released the pigeon. Ben heard its little wings beating in the air. He saw the pigeon fly over head and he knew it was on its way home.

Dad had arrived home. He went to the back of the house to check all his pigeons had flown in safely. He counted them into their little nesting boxes. He thought he had all of them, but as he got to the end of the nesting boxes he realised one was empty. One bird had not returned. Ben's dad was very upset about that. He wanted all his birds back in their nests. He decided to wait a few more minutes. Then Rusty arrived. Dad greeted Rusty and gave him a pat. Ben's dad looked up expecting to see Ben with Rusty, but Ben was not there. Dad shook his head and was sure Ben was already inside the house having tea with mom in the kitchen.

Dad waited a few more minutes for the missing bird. He heard the whirring sound of wings. He saw the last bird coming in. The bird seemed anxious and flew round and round the room. It did not want to go into its box. Dad put out his arm to see if the bird would come to him. The bird flew down and landed on dad's outstretched hand. Then dad saw something tied to the pigeon's foot. The carrier pigeon was carrying something different. It was not one of dad's messages or notes from the competition. Dad unwound the string and put the pigeon back in its nesting box.

Meanwhile Ben was sitting waiting and wondering if the pigeon had flown back to the house to give dad the unusual message. A piece of thread from his track suit.

When dad got inside he realised Ben was not there. He showed the string to mom and she recognised it straight away.

"It's a thread from Ben's track suit," said mom. "I wonder how the pigeon got it tied to its foot?"

Dad knew there was something wrong. He wondered if the pigeon would lead the way back to where Ben was. Then there was Rusty too. He should know the way.

"I am going to get the pigeon and take Rusty too. We must find Ben," said dad.

Dad took out the pigeon and showed it the thread. The pigeon cocked its head and then took off in the direction of the hills and the caves. Dad was pleased to have eyes in the air and Rusty's eyes on the ground. Dad felt glad he had such a great search and rescue team.

The pigeon flew ahead and Rusty followed to the place where Ben was trapped. The pigeon flew down and sat on the branch and Rusty started barking. When Ben heard the barking he called out to his dad. Ben's dad went forward carefully with a rope to let down for Ben. Slowly Ben was brought to the top of the hole.

Dad gave Ben a big hug he was so glad to see him. They waved at the pigeon flying back to the house. Ben his dad and Rusty went home after an amazing rescue adventure.

Chapter 20: Down a rabbit hole

Ruth loved reading. She read before school and after school and at the weekend. Her friends called her the class bookworm. Ruth did not mind being called a bookworm. She enjoyed it because it gave her all the more excuse to sit and read.

One day Ruth was reading in the garden. She was reading a well known book called Alice and Wonderland. She had read it before, but she loved the characters in the story. Ruth especially loved the White Rabbit. She wondered what it would be like to follow a rabbit down his hole like Alice did. It was quite a hot day when Ruth was reading her book. Ruth lent back on the tree trunk where she was sitting and fell asleep. Suddenly she woke up to a pattering sound.

Ruth opened one eye and then the other. Then she rubbed both eyes to check if she was not seeing things. She saw a rabbit, a white rabbit hopping in front of her. Ruth could not believe this picture. The white rabbit stopped in front of Ruth and started to shake its head. It looked at Ruth and started to talk.

"Excuse me little girl," said the white rabbit.

Ruth just sat with her mouth open and stared.

"Excuse me little girl. Can you help me to the nearest rabbit hole?" asked the white rabbit.

Ruth shook her head, she had not seen a rabbit hole in the garden.

"Well, you are a silly girl," said the rabbit. It tutted in an annoying way and started to walk off.

Ruth did not want to be called silly by a rabbit so she called after the rabbit.

"Sorry rabbit, perhaps I can help you to find one?" suggested Ruth.

The rabbit stopped for a minute and then nodded its head and beckoned for Ruth to follow. Ruth was not sure about following a rabbit, but follow him she did. Then suddenly the rabbit disappeared and so did Ruth. She felt the earth falling beneath her. Down and down fell Ruth and finally she landed with a bump.

There were many little bunnies running along the track that led in front of her. All the rabbits had little bags on their backs and they were in a hurry. Finally Ruth managed to stop one of the rabbits.

"Where are you going?" asked Ruth.

The little rabbit was quite out of breath.

"We are off to school. Come on or you will be late," said the rabbit.

Ruth looked very surprised. Rabbits going to school? She decided to follow the rabbits because really she did not know what else to do. All the little rabbits ran and ran to the gates of a big school. They ran into the school yard as the bell rang for school to start.

All the little rabbits lined up and a big rabbit came to the top of the school stairs.

"Hop to it everyone," said the big rabbit. Everyone went hopping along the corridors to get to their classrooms. Ruth followed along too. She did not hop. She just walked along slowly and found a desk to sit at.

She was sitting next to a very annoying rabbit that kept tap tapping its foot on the floor under the desk. Then Ruth heard a loud crunching noise behind her. She turned round to see a rabbit munching on a carrot. This was turning into a crazy classroom.

The first lesson was about Boadicea the Bunny Queen who led an army against the Romans. Ruth could not believe her eyes as a picture of a rabbit riding a chariot was on the first page of the history book.

"You see rabbits made history! We were part of the first battles against the enemy the Romans," said the teacher.

Ruth tried to pay attention but all the while the lesson was on the rabbits in the classroom were misbehaving and not listening. They were munching on carrots and eating lettuce leaves. At last it was time for a lunch break. Ruth went outside with all the bunnies. She wondered what they would do during their recess time.

It was time to play hopscotch of course. Ruth nodded her head as she saw all the bunnies hopping on the hopscotch games. Suddenly Ruth saw the rabbit she had followed. He was anxiously crossing the playground. Ruth decided she should follow him because she did not know how she was going to get back home. It was all very well to follow a rabbit down a rabbit hole, but Ruth had decided it was time for this adventure to be over.

She caught up with the rabbit and tapped him politely on his shoulder. He turned round and looked at her with a puzzled expression.

"Excuse me," said Ruth politely. "Can you help me find my way back to my garden?"

"Well if you want to go back. You have to go back. Backwards. Walk backwards the way you came," said the rabbit.

Ruth looked really puzzled at that idea. She had no choice but to copy the rabbit and start to walk backwards. She hoped that it took her home. She was so busy walking backwards that she didn't notice she had bumped into something else on the path, The path back home to her garden.

"Ouch," came a little voice. Ruth looked everywhere, but she couldn't see anything. She was about to carry on walking backwards when she heard the little voice again.

"What are you doing walking backwards?" said the voice.

"I am trying to get back home to my garden," answered Ruth.

"Well why don't you turn round and walk back?" said the voice.

Ruth looked down again and there on the path she saw a wriggly worm. The worm had little spectacles on the end of its nose and had a book under its front legs. It was an inch worm that had funny feet at the top of its body and then more feet at the bottom.

"Hi. I am Billy Bookworm," said the worm as it looked up at Ruth.

Ruth looked down amazed. Was there really such a thing as a bookworm. Clearly in this strange place there was a bookworm. Ruth turned round to get a closer look. Then she looked up and realised that she could really walk back along the path without walking backwards.

"How silly of me," said Ruth.

The bookworm just nodded. Ruth walked along and the bookworm wriggled down the path with her. What a funny sight they made. Ruth was glad to have the bookworm beside her because it seemed far more sensible that the silly rabbits.

"So what are your favorite books?" asked the bookworm.

"I love all kinds of books, but my favorite story has always been Alice in Wonderland," said Ruth. Then she looked a bit sad.

"You don't seem to be happy about that one right now," said the bookworm.

"Well, you see I wanted to know what it felt like to be down a rabbit hole," said Ruth.

Then Ruth explained to the bookworm how she had fallen asleep under a tree and somehow a rabbit had hopped by and she had followed the rabbit. Ruth carried on telling her story about the rabbits and rabbit school. It was all very strange and fun at first but then it became silly and annoying.

"I couldn't find my way home until a rabbit told me to walk backwards," said Ruth.

The bookworm giggled. Ruth could tell he understood how she felt. After all he was a book worm. He knew about interesting stories and imagination.

"I really want to get home now," said Ruth, as she began to climb some crooked stairway. She was sure she could see a light at the top of the stairs. The stairs led up to some bushes. Ruth pushed the bushes aside and there, in front of her, was the garden. Ruth was so relieved she flopped down on the grass and closed her eyes. She wanted to be sure that when she opened them again she was really at home.

"Ruth where are you?" called a voice.

It was her mom calling from the kitchen. Ruth opened her eyes and blinked twice. There were no rabbits around. She breathed a sigh of relief. Then she saw her book. It was lying on the grass. Ruth picked up the book and she laughed out loud. Sitting on the book was a little inch worm. She watched it take a few steps forward and then let its body catch up moving inch by inch.

"Hello little worm," said Ruth as she gently took it over to the bushes and let it go on a leaf.

"Who are you talking to?" asked her mom.

"Oh just a little bookworm who helped me find my way home," said Ruth. Her mom laughed and muttered something about Ruth and her fantasy books.

Conclusion

I am a parent myself. So, I have seen the moralizing effect of bedtime stories. And I know how morality is priceless, and how humanizing it is. We are their basic means of socialization. The values that we instill in them, they carry them throughout their lives.

Even you and I, maybe unaware, still carry so many ideas from our childhood. Many of us who had somebody tell us bedtime tales; we often give into nostalgia, and remember the voices telling us of a certain knightly prince and his brave mare. Hence, I deem bedtime stories valuable in so many ways.

To me, the fundamental reason behind my motivation to develop the perfect set of stories is these very moral values. I have struggled to perceive such, and in the way, it became my passion. My life's passion has taken shape in the form of a book through which I hope to serve any parents who are looking to mold the creative and wonderful minds of their children.

Finally, if you found this book useful in any way, a review on Amazon is always appreciated! Thank you and all the best!

Sarah

Bedtime Stories For Kids -2-

A Unique Short Stories Collection for Toddlers and Children to Help them Fall Asleep Soundly and Avoid Long Bedtime Battles. Drift Off to Dreamland with Magical Creatures

Ingrid Connor

Introduction

It has been a tiring day for you and your child. All you seek right now in the comfort of your bed. While your child still wants to play with you. This is a perfect time. Bring out a book of bedtime stories. Your child still has your company, and you don't have to run around with him to play.

Reading out bedtime stories to your child can become a great routine for you to bond. It can help both of you wind down and relax. Leave behind all the woes and worries, shed down all the stress and tension, and together float away into fantasy. Just like you might like sleeping to audiobooks, music, or certain nature sounds.

I have found that bedtime stories work great for children. Washing down all the negative emotions, your child can imagine a world so colorful and happy. A world above the clouds. A world not human, and maybe they are the king of the forest.

Bedtime stories open your child to so many interesting ideas and so many new worlds. They help your child imagine. They let your child dream. Muhammad Ali once said, "The man who has no imagination has no wings." Cut down their wings, and they stop growing. For, bedtime stories send your child to a world where they can create, where they can empathize with the wounded deer, and they can be happy for the excited bear who found his honey. Bedtime stories are a great catalyst for your child to develop with the right emotional and mental intelligence. They mature and start getting a hint about the world's machinery. They learn about consequences.

They start creating their endings to the stories and might even foresee the correct ending. Send your child off to a beautiful, dreamy world made of cotton with beautiful bedtime tales, and not to a world of ghouls.

Chapter 1: Sammy's Space Adventure

Every night before bed, Sammy loves to read. Books are his best friends, and especially those about space. He is interested in this large vastness since he was a little boy. Since the moment he received a big illustrated book about space for his fifth birthday, he knew he would have a lot of fun reading it. The book was full of colorful pictures. There were all the planets in our solar system, comets, asteroids, galaxies and of course the Sun. Sammy is especially fond of Mars because red is his favorite color. He knows all there is to know about this planet. Still, he likes to fantasize the most. Sammy simply loves to imagine what life on Mars would look like. His eyes light up when he talks about his precious planet. Tonight is no different than any other previous night. Sammy went to bed, snuck in with his Mars book, and embarked on a new adventure. Pictures shuffled before his eyes. They looked so gleaming and colorful. Under his fingers, he felt the smooth surface of the Mars image and sighed deeply.

- "Oh, how I wish to go to Mars. I hope one day the astronauts will find a way for me to do it. "

Little, curious eyes then closed and Sammy sank into the dream. Hands rested still on the book, touching its silky texture. In his mind, a movie began to unfold, in which he is the hero. A Mars movie.

A ray of light flashed through the children's room window and the curtains parted. Followed by the flashing lights and a weird beeping sound, a small flying saucer flew into the room. Operating in a small space was not easy, so the stranger stopped eventually in the open closet, causing a loud thud.

- "Huh, what happened?" Sammy jumped out of bed awake from sleep. He looked around with tired eyes around the room, trying to get used to the light. He was attracted to an even bigger mess in the closet than the one he left behind. There was some creaking noise, and then hissing of steam which filled up the room. The quiet melodic repetition of the tones came from the closet. Something was walking towards Sammy wearing a shirt of the school's basketball team. Wait a minute, a walking shirt? Sammy boldly stepped forward and grabbed the soft material of his shirt. A small red creature stood in front of him, staring at him in wonder.

- "Hey, you're not green!" Sammy screeched

- "Hey, neither are you!" replied the alien, "Who are you?"

- "I'm Sammy, and you're in my room. Are you going to tell me who you are? I know you're an alien, but what planet are you from? "

- "I am Marty Martian and I should not be here. I've heard that there is someone on your Earth who knows all about my Mars, so I came to seek help. "

-"I know all about Mars," Sammy said enthusiastically

- "Really? Um, I was expecting someone higher than you."

- "Hey, look at me, I know I'm the only boy who knows this much about Mars. My appearance has nothing to do with it."

-"Really? I need someone very brave to go through the field of mist to save our queen. "

- "Mars has a queen?" The look on Sammy's face was priceless. He knew absolutely everything about this planet, but he had no idea that Mars has a queen. For heaven's sake, he didn't even know that Mars had real, existing Martians.

- "Oh, forget it, you don't seem to know all about Mars."I'm going to look for someone who can really help me." Marty said in a squeaky tone. His eyes looked so sad and disappointed.

- "Look, Marty, I may not have known you had a queen, but I believed in my heart and felt that life on Mars existed. Let me come with you and help my favorite planet."

- "Okay, Sammy. I believe you have a good soul and a pure heart. I feel that you are the one who will help Queen Martina. Come on, my spaceship will take us to Mars. The flight is really fast, like lightning."

Indeed, as soon as they boarded Marty's spaceship, there was a creaking sound of metal and the engine started humming. In a split second, they flew and disappeared from the face of the earth with a thunderbolt explosion. Landing on Mars was smooth and steady. As soon as they stepped out of the spaceship Sammy stopped stood in the place. He seemed to be frozen, but a storm of emotions whirled inside of him. He is finally on his favorite planet! Sammy looked like he loves Mars more than he loves Earth. The boy blinked rapidly as his eyes adjusted to the daylight on Mars. He definitely isn't in his room anymore. Everywhere around him were hills covered in powdery red dust.

There was air, despite what his books taught him. There was a sky, but its clouds were crimson and fluffy. Mars wasn't scary at all. The planet felt warm and welcoming. Marty made the first step and Sammy followed him.

- "Do you like it on Mars, Sammy?" Marty was eagerly awaiting his response

"Yes, very ..." Sammy only managed to say those words before a misty veil formed in front of him.

- "Hurry up, Sammy. Mars is beautiful, but we don't have time to waste. Only you can get past this curtain. It is dangerous for us Martians. The queen sits atop a sand dune."

Sammy left without any questions. As he ran the soft sand moved under his feet leaving prints behind him. He ran through the haze which began tickling his nose. It smelled like fresh spring morning full of dew. The boy was surprised. Then he took a deep breath and inhaled that scent that gave him more energy. The Queen should not be far away. He had already been running for a few minutes and hoped the sand dunes are nearby. Just when it seemed like he couldn't take it anymore, Sammy tripped and fell nose-first into the powdery sand. The words echoed in his mind that he must save the Queen. This boy was very brave, so he stood up and shook the red sand gains of sand off his clothes and hair.

- "I have to move on."

The strength did not leave him, so Sammy arrived soon at the magnificent sight. In front of him was a large desert in various shades of red. On the largest dune, he saw someone sitting and crying. Silent sobs were reached Sammy and made him sad. It seemed like the boy himself would cry.

-"That must be the queen." he thought.

With a new rush of stamina, Sammy started climbing the largest sand dune. The sand beneath him was slippery and slid through his fingers. He felt its pleasant warmth.

"My queen," Sammy panted as he finally climbed to the top. "I came to save you."

Queen Martina stopped crying immediately and asked in a hushed voice.

-        - "Who are you, boy? I'm not your queen, you come from Earth. And I'm not coming back. I don't need a rescue. Go away!" The queen wrinkled her little red nose and her cheeks got dark red like cherries. She looked like a little girl.

-        - "I am Sammy. Yes, I come from Earth, but I'm here because I want to help Mars. I really love Mars. I don't want the Martians to be sad because their queen is missing."

-        - "How do you not understand Sammy? I ran away on my own because I was bored with being a queen on this planet. I want to be free and travel space. Mars has nothing more to offer me."

-        - "Oh, you are so wrong, my Queen. Mars is beautiful. I know all about it. But I didn't know the air was so pleasant here. It smells like beautiful spring flowers. The ground is soft and velvety. I can't get hurt anywhere if I fall. It's gentle, very gentle. Everywhere I turn my head I hear a soothing song sung by Martians. When was the last time you looked at Mars? As we approached it, I saw a beautiful red planet. I've never seen such a beautiful shade of color in my life. Mars is breathtaking" I'm sure if you look at your home again you will love it. I only saw one part but it looks incredible to me. So, what do you say Queen Martina? Will you come back with me?"

\-   - "You're right Sammy, Mars is beautiful. Yes, I'll come with you. I have no heart to leave such a beautiful place. I feel so safe and happy here."

\-   - "Me too, my Queen. I feel like Mars is my second home. I love Earth, but I really like it here. Can I come back and visit you?"

\-   - "Of course, Sammy. But first, I have to take you to the teleport station. We need to get you home to bed.

The queen clapped her hands and they both turned up in a beautiful room with only one bed in the middle.

\-   "Come on, Sammy, go to bed. As soon as you fall asleep we will teleport you back to Earth."

Sammy climbed onto a bed that was soft as a cloud. The blanket was as warm as the first summer sun rays and it smelled clean. It smelled like home. The Martians' lullaby started again and Sammy began to sink into sleep. He felt his body become relaxed, and he thought he was wandering the vast expanses of Mars. He saw red dunes again and almost felt the velvety sand under his hands. A smile appeared on his face and Sammy fell asleep. He dreamed of returning to Earth, his colorful books

about space and his mother's soft lips kissing him goodnight.
Mars was saved, and Sammy happy and content.

Chapter 2: Amy's New Friends

The little blond girl was lying under a massive oak tree. Her hair fell around her like a soft hug. It was a lovely sunny day. The birds were chirping a pleasant melody somewhere among the branches. Amy inhaled and exhaled. She felt peaceful in nature. The late spring was welcoming summer with fields full of colorful flowers and warm sun rays. It looked like the whole animal kingdom was out and about. Amy smiled as her cat stretched and purred with pleasure. She loved spending time on this meadow. It smelled florally and fresh. Many different flowers were scattered across the field. They created a lovely mosaic and played a fun game with the wind and bees. Nature was alive in spring. Among these sounds and movements, Amy thought she heard something strange. It sounded like someone was crying. Just when she got up to explore, her eyes caught a glimpse of something moving in the tall grass.

- "Come, Fluffy, let's see what that is."

The sweet child's voice was rining as Amy's blue dress rustled with each step. The tall leaves of grass were smooth against her skin. She was focused on the thumping sound coming from the grass. As she moved closer, Amy noticed it's a little bunny making that sound. It looked like the bunny is sad and afraid. His little eyes were bursting with tears. The bunny had one of his velvety ears in his paws and was looking at Amy.

- "Hello, little fellow. What's the matter?"

Amy loved animals. She didn't want any of them to be hurt. Her melodic voice calmed the bunny immediately.

-"I am lost. I don't know my way back home. I feel so sad." The little bunny looked like he was about to start crying again.

-"Don't be sad, little bunny. I will help you find your family. My cat Fluffy will help too."

Amy sat down in the grass and put the bunny in her lap. Her fingers gave the best tummy-rubs and ear-scratches. Fluffy sat next to her watching the bunny. It looked like it's the first time he saw one in person. Fluffy loved other animals too, even dogs. He was kind just like his owner, Amy.

-"If I have a name, Amy, then he must have one too." Fluffy was proud of his finding. He was one smart kitty.

-"You are right, Fluffy," answered Amy, "Tell us your name, little guy," Amy asked kindly.

-"I'm Cotton Tail. I am pleased to meet you two. Now, could you please help me find my family? They will be worried if I don't come home before the dark." The bunny looked worried. Amy couldn't stand to see him down.

-"You are one very polite bunny, Cotton Tail. Of course, we'll help you out. Do you remember where your family lives?"

-"It's by the river, under the big willow tree. We just moved there, but it feels like home and smells so sweet. The river is sparkling clean and there's a lot of food to eat and interesting places to explore. Oh, I wish I was there right now." The bunny's shoulders lowered in sadness as he remembered his home.

-"Come on, let's get you home. I don't want you to feel sad anymore."

Three friends crossed the vibrant meadow and headed down the path towards the reflecting water. The bunny hopped happily trying to keep up the pace. He was excited to see his mom, dad, and five brothers and sisters. The birds followed them singing their captivating song and small critters watched the merry company with interest. Little by little, squirrels, hedgehogs, and other tiny forest animals joined in.

-"We want to help out too!"

-"Come with us," said Amy, "it's better when friends stay together."

An interesting company of one girl, a cat, a bunny, and a bunch of forest animals went over the wooden bridge. The road was getting bumpy and the daylight got dimmed. There was no brightness coming from the sun anymore.

-"Oh, no, it looks like it's going to rain. Guys, we have to hurry!", Amy shrieked in fright.

Just when they hurried the pace, something made a rustling sound behind them.

-"Where are you guys going?", a thundering voice echoed.

A large bear stood before them. He was twice as tall as Amy. The bear's fur wasn't fluffy and silky as it should be. It looked like he fell in the mud and it smelled musty too. But, his eyes weren't scary at all. They were large, round and warm.

-"We're taking the bunny home, mister bear. How can we help you?" Amy answered politely.

-"I am one sad bear. I fell in the mud when I was trying to get some honey. The bees stung me and now my paw hurts. Other bears won't be my friends. They laugh at me because I'm a bit clumsy. Everywhere I go you hear thuds and stomps. My only wish is to have friends. I'm not that frightening, am I? Will you guys be my friends?" The bear's eyes looked awfully sad. He let a gloomy sigh and bowed down his head.

Amy looked at her company of friends. All the animals were looking at her with approval. Their heart was kind. She knew it's the right thing to accept this bear as their friend.

-"Of course we'll be your friends. I am Amy, this is my cat Fluffy and this here is Cotton Tail. We're bringing him home."

-"I'm Smokey the bear and I'm very happy to meet you all. You are my first friends ever. I will take care of you in case the big, bad wolf comes."

Smokey was excited he made new friends who don't judge him or the way his fur looks. He believed he's a good bear.

Amy and her animal friends continued their mission. It's almost dinner time and Cotton Tail is still not home. His family must be worried sick.

-"Come, friends, let's hurry. If we don't get Cotton Tail back to his home it will get dark and cold." Amy proclaimed and hastened.

The animals followed her and they were soon on the right path. The willow tree was near. They went down the river and found themselves in front of a lovely rabbit hole. A garden patch full of carrots was next to the hole and the heavenly smell was spreading out. Freshly washed bunny clothes were hanging off a wire. The entrance in the hole was neatly decorated with wildflowers and colorful stones. It looked like a true family home. The bunnies were surely having a wonderful life in their new home.

-"That's my home, and that yummy smell is my mom's carrot cake! I'm home! Thank you, Amy. Thanks, everyone, for helping me."

Cotton Tail's happiness couldn't be measured. He hopped quickly to his home, calling for his mom and dad. He was finally home, in his parent's embrace. They were relieved their son came home safely. All the little bunny brothers and sisters were thrilled Cotton Tail was home.

-"Cotton Tail didn't mean to wander off, but he was lucky to find you, Amy. Me and mommy bunny thank you all. Would you like to stay for a slice of carrot cake?" Daddy bunny expressed his gratitude by offering cake.

The company was delighted. They ate cake and told stories. Amy never thought she would have so much fun talking with forest animals. She already loved every single one of them. She loved the cake too! Even Smokey the bear tried carrot cake and loved it.

-"Hmm, I love this treat as much as I love my honey! Smokey said enthusiastically.

Everyone laughed. Happiness was almost touchable.

The day was coming to an end. Amy had to go home before her mother becomes worried too. She was afraid she would get lost in the dark.

-"Fluffy, we need to go now. I am really happy I met you all today. We did a good deed by helping Cotton Tail and we made new friends. Isn't this a day well spent?"

The animals nodded and cheered at Amy. She promised she will come back every day for a slice of carrot cake and to share a laugh with Smokey, squirrels, hedgehogs, Cotton Tail and his bunny family. Smokey accompanied Fluffy and Amy home and once again said his thanks.

-"Amy, you're a wonderful little girl. Thank you for everything. See you again tomorrow in the meadow?"

-"It was my pleasure, Smokey. We'll see you tomorrow, and we'll bring you some honey."

The bear smiled and waved goodbye.

That night, Amy and Fluffy fell asleep hugged and blissful. It looked like they both were smiling in their dreams.

As he was drifting into dreamland himself, Cotton Tail's eyes sparkled with happiness again: he realized he made friends for life today. That was enough to help him sail through the cotton clouds of the dreams.

Everything was good now. Everything was peaceful.

Chapter 3: What lies behind the rainbow?

Have you ever wondered what lies behind the rainbow? We all see the rainbow. It's a beautiful miracle coming after the rain. Sometimes our eyes can't see it, but that doesn't stop us from imagining. Let's conjure a rainbow together. Come on, close your eyes. Pretend the quick summer rain has just ended. The air smells so fresh, doesn't it? Nature awakes for the second time today. It looks like the rain came like a blessing. Heavy clouds are dispersed across the sky. The sun is shining through and chasing bad weather. The divine rainbow is now ruling the sky.

Look at the colorful arch. It's standing proudly and stealing delighted sighs. The warm red color dominates the rainbow. It looks like a sweet, juicy apple, freshly picked from the tree. The orange follows and lures with its vibrancy. Yellow is a happy color that puts a smile on the face immediately. It reminds of soft dandelions sprinkled on the green grass. The rainbow's green is just like the grass itself. It invites you to enjoy nature's blessings. Light blue is soft and fluffy like the clouds of cotton candy sold on the carnival. Next to her flashes indigo; the dark blue shade of the deepest sea. You can almost hear the waves smashing against the rocks. Purple is smiling at you charmingly. She stole the prettiest color from the violets. Oh, she almost smells like violets too!

The magic of the rainbow goes by quickly. Soak up the beauty before it disappears. If you want to enjoy more beauty, then, go to the place where the rainbow ends. You will find it if your will is strong and your heart clean. There lies a pot full of gold and a leprechaun smiling at you. He's inviting you to come with him. The magic of the rainbow didn't vanish. The little leprechaun dressed in a green suit holds your hand and takes you on an adventure. A sprinkle of magic dust from his hat gets you two in a place you've never been before. As your eyes adapt to the bright scene you realize you've crossed into another realm. Magic of the rainbow guards this valley like the very best secret. Hear the bells echoing loudly in the valley. There are cows on the field behind you greeting you with mooing and bell-ringing. Their sounds create a wonderful symphony. But cows aren't the only musicians behind the rainbow. The ducks are flying by and making a performance for you. Hear their quacking. Do you realize how happy they are to see you? You smile and wave at the animals. Sprinkled across the valley are trees with voluminous treetops. The birds are chirping in the branches and inviting you to come closer. Their song is hypnotizing. You hear many different tones and recognize multiple bird species. This valley is very abundant. Your step is light and the grass soft as if you're stepping on cotton buds. Careful, don't hurt the gentle buds. The colorful flowers are everywhere around you. The opulent scents and pollen are mixing in the air and making your body relaxed and light as a feather. You hum as you hear the buzzing noise coming from the bees. It feels like the whole valley is vibrating from their sounds. The bees fly around you, but they won't hurt you. The touch of their wings is silky smooth. The place behind the rainbow channels inner peace. You can't decide on which side to go first. On your right, there is a lake, so clear that the clouds are reflecting in it. On your left, you see a swing made of entwined flowers.

The merry leprechaun is sitting by the lake and calling you to come near. He is delighted with the new visitor in his world.

-"Come, sit with me. The lake is a wonderful place to refresh your tired body. Look, it's shining like a gemstone. I love looking at the lake. It changes colors with each time of the day. The morning brings a deep shade of red. As the sun rises the lake becomes blue as the sky and beautiful like the fines sapphire. The evening is my favorite part. The water gets the shade of blood orange. I bet if I taste it the taste will citrusy. All this beauty is priceless. The trees have dressed gorgeous green tops. The birds have learned a new song in your honor. They have the prettiest voices to listen to. Their melody is spreading across the valley gently, but still captivating. Listen carefully. You might never hear anything so beautiful again. It's not difficult to enjoy such a divine place. The body surrenders to the peace and quiet, and the sleep is sneaking in like a thief in the night. You are feeling tired, aren't you? The trip to the end of the rainbow is long, but it worth the trouble when you see all this beauty. Come, I want you to rest and try our hammock. Feel how gentle the flowers are of which it's made. They're soothing against your skin. Inhale the scents which spread and take over your body and soul. I hope you're comfortable lying there. It looks like the best place to fall asleep. Fresh air, lovely music and swinging are the secret recipe for a tranquil nap. Allow me to push you slowly. Left and then right. Left and right again. The summer breeze is helping too! You just relax your body and allow me to send you to the magical land of dreams."

You feel how your body becomes numb. Your thoughts are drifting away. Suddenly, you see yourself lying in a gorgeous floral hammock. Tiny animals are watching you sleep as the birds are singing a tuneful lullaby. You are flying above them. You realize you're having an out-of-body experience. Goosebumps are running on your skin. A tingling feeling builds on your back. A pair of magnificent, velvety white wings has grown on you. They carry you as you fly over the rainbow's valley. You see an endless space of untouched and unspoiled nature. Over the hill lies the other part of the valley, more beautiful than the one you first saw. You get lower and cruise above the magnificent orchard. The trees are fruitful and you can almost taste the sweet apples and pears. Their juice is inviting you to come down and quench your thirst. As soon as you land on the grass your wings disappear. They fold softly behind you and leave a powdery trace. It looks like they were sent from the heavenly angels. It was nice having them for a while. Flying gave you a sense of power. But,

There is no more time to think of the wings. New and undiscovered parts of the second valley are calling your name. You hear it like a whisper between the branches. As you lift your head there's a shiny red apple hanging in front of your eyes. You touch its silky skin and grasp it firmly. The smell is divine and filling your mouth with water. The first bite activates all your taste buds. It's luscious and invites you to take another bite. This is not a forbidden apple from the story. It's an apple from rainbow's valley made to satisfy you and give energy before the next adventure.

Your body is full now, but your eyes are still hungry for picturesque sights. There is more than this beautiful orchard. A lovely hummingbird buzzes before you. It looks like it wants you to follow it. You go after the hummingbird between the lines of identical trees which lead to you to a clearing. The bird disappears with a silent poof. In front of you is a deep river coming down from a steep mountain. The water murmurs as it hits rocks. It's glistening clear. You come near and sit on the riverside. The day is pleasantly warm, so you decide to refresh yourself. First, your feet stir up the running water. The little fishes in the shallow water greet you with nibbling your toes. It feels ticklish but still nice. The sun begins to fry from above. You see the river as an escape from the heath. Soon, you find yourself dipped in the cold water. Your body gets an instant boost of energy as you swim down the stream. Let the river carry you. Relax your muscles and surrender to the velvety touch of the water. You drift away as the water runs towards its end on the horizon. The river finds the sea and mixes with the salty water as one. You're now a part of a deep sea. Dolphins and fishes swim by you as you float. The salty water doesn't let you sink. You're lighter than air and have never been more carefree in your life. The sea is peaceful. You're peaceful. You are one with the sea.

Chapter 4: The little dinosaur that couldn't sleep

Once upon a time, when you were not born yet, there was a little dinosaur. He was called Scully and he was the favourite one in the herbivore valley. All the other dinosaurs loved his blue skin, smooth and glowy like jewels. He lived happily with his mom, dad, and sister Sandy. The little family loved to spend days nibbling on delicious leaves and bathing in freshwater. Scully was a good little dinosaur. But one evening, a small problem happened. When all the dinosaurs of the valley went to sleep, Scully couldn't. He turned left and right, thinking of the day that had passed, imagining the next one, but nothing could put him to sleep. Eventually, he decided to call his mom. Mom told Scully a story with much of love. That made him relaxed for a few moments. But still, the sleep was not coming.

- "Mom, tell me another story, please." Little Scully begged his mother. He looked so sad, so Mom felt sorry for him and told an even longer story.

- "But Mom, I'm still not sleepy. What should we do now?" Scully was persistent

- "Let's count the stars together. That will put you to sleep. " Mom smiled kindly and showed Scully to look up at the night sky.

The night was cloudless and peaceful and the sky dark. Gleaming stars were placed all over it. They looked like little sparkly flowers scattered across the sky. Scully counted one by one as the stars in his large eyes flickered and dazzled even more. It seemed as if new stars were constantly appearing in the sky. Scully enjoyed the game of dancing lights in the sky. He wondered where the stars were going when the big ball, that the adults call the sun, appears. The breeze gently stirred the tree's branches carrying the smell of grass from afar. The picture of Scully watching the magnificent stars was beautiful to Scully's mom. The dinosaur mother fell asleep hugging her little boy. Scully, tucked under mom's neck, inhaled the smell of his mother and enjoyed the warmth her hug gave to him. However, the dream was nowhere in sight.

"Mom," Scully whispered, "I still can't sleep. What should I do?" The worried face of the little dinosaur appeared before his Mom's eyes.

- "Okay, child, don't worry, we'll find a way for you to go to sleep. Look at our valley. It's beautiful, isn't it? There is a lot of fresh grass and many different trees. Come on, why don't you count which plants we all know and love to eat? " Mom kissed Scully softly and placed him beside her to try to go to sleep again.

"Um," Scully thought to himself, "there are many plants I know. It will surely put me to sleep. "

Scully smiled and closed his weary eyes. He was very tired, but something wouldn't let him sleep. The plants were lined up, one after the other. It seemed to Scaly that he could eat them now. They smelled tempting in his head and almost appeared like they were in front of him. Then a strange grumble was heard. It was Scully's stomach. The little dinosaur was starving from thinking of all that food. He shook his sleepy mom and called her:

- "Mom, I'm hungry. I can't sleep hungry. "

- "Oh, child, you're still not sleeping? Let's see what we can do about that hungry belly. " Mommy dinosaur's forehead wrinkled and her face looked worried. Scaly never had a problem with sleeping. She'll have to find something to eat quickly.

Mom went in search of the leaves that everyone ate that day. They tasted delightful. The little Scully was looking for her, eagerly awaiting her return. The joy on his face was obvious when Mom returned carrying many fleshy leaves.

- "Thanks, Mom. I'll definitely fall asleep as soon as I eat some. "

Scully threw himself at the food. The large, smooth leaves were very thick and juicy. They smelled appetizing. Scully ate one at a time until he ate them all. He smiled happily and turned to his mom.

- "They were very tasty, mom. I'm going to sleep now. "

The little dinosaur happily went back to his place. Behind him was his mom hugging him with her tail to keep him warm. Mom's soft skin gave comfort and Scully snuggled.

- "One, two, three ... I'm sure to fall asleep now."

Scully blinked slowly and muttered, calling sleep to come to him. The sounds of his whispers waked his sister Sandy. The little sister stretched and walked over the silky grass that was already sprinkled with dew.

- "Scully, what's the matter? Why aren't you sleeping?" Sandy asked with a concerned look on her face

- "I don't know, Sandy. Help me. What do you do when you can't sleep? "

- "Oh, that's easy: I go catching fireflies. The game always makes me tired and I fall asleep immediately afterwards. " Sandy said proudly

- "And where are those fireflies?" her brother asked curiously

- "Down there, by the river. Come on, I'll take you. Just make sure Mom doesn't hear us.

Two little dinosaurs sneaked from mom and dad to go to the river. Under their feet, the pebbles creaked and bounced. They followed their footsteps until they reached the river. The surface of the water was calm and dark. The stars reflected in it, and the moon joined in on the party too. The river shimmered like the brightest star from the sky. A swarm of fireflies played next to one bush. The warm, yellow lights went on and off. Scully and Sandy watched their dance with admiration. The fireflies went up, down, left and right, and then circled around them. One landed on Scully's nose. He could feel the warmth of its light, and he held in his laugh because it tickled him. That prickly movement of the firefly did not last long. Something rustled behind them and the fireflies scattered. The heavy steps vibrated the ground when a low voice echoed.

- "Hey, Scully and Sandy. You can't sleep either? "

It was their friend Buddy, a big dinosaur who was constantly making noises, squeaking and chewing on leaves. That one was always hungry!

"Hey, Buddy. What do you do when you can't sleep?" asked Scully, "I'm very tired, but nothing works. Not counting, not food, not fireflies. " Scully already looked blue. His eyes gazed sadly at the floor.

- "I know what you need, Scully. A little fresh water! I came for that too. "Buddy walked boldly to the river. He seemed so proud that he had come up with a way to make Scully sleep.

Little dinosaur Scully got down and started drinking water. A sip, two, three and it was enough. Although the water was so pleasing and refreshing, he couldn't drink anymore.

- "Buddy, I don't think this works either." Said Scully with frustration

-"I have an idea! How about we run in circles? That should get you tired. I always fall asleep when I run a little. "Buddy smiled

- "No, Buddy, Scully's tired. He can't run now. He needs some magical sleeping solution. "

- "Hmm, I really don't know anything anymore. It's best to go to your mom. She always knows what to do. " Buddy said cheerfully, and with the sounds of the breaking twigs, moved away from the brother and sister.

- "Yes, Mom will know for sure!" Sandy confirmed and nudged his brother to go back.

Scaly didn't have a good feeling. Mom didn't help the first few times. What if nothing will work again?

- "Hey, Mom. I still can't sleep." He whispered to his mother's ear

- "Neither do I, Mom," Sandy added quietly on the other one

The mother dinosaur woke from her dream and looked at her children. An idea came to her immediately.

- "This will work, I'm sure." The mother thought to herself and gave the children the warmest smile

- "Sandy, Scully, come and give me a hug. Your mother will sing a lullaby now. "

As she gently swung her children, the dinosaur mother hummed. Melodic sounds spread across the valley and reached the ears of other dinosaurs. The catchy song created a sense of love and security in Scully and Sandy. Mom smelled like home. Mom smelled like happiness. Every now and then she would kiss Scully and Sandy. The rhythmic swing sent the little ones into the land of dreams. They fell asleep quickly. They dreamed of fireflies and mom and dad playing with them by the river. The smile looked glued to their faces. Before falling asleep, Scully realized that not the stars, plants, fireflies, nor water could replace his mother's touch. It was as gentle as silk and as light as a feather. Mom is a haven that is always there when we need her.

Chapter 5: The boy who spoke to animals

Noah's father was a veterinarian. He had a small office on the main street of their town. Everyone loved Dr. Brown and happily brought their pets for a checkup. There were various animals: dogs, cats, guinea pigs, hamsters, and even one ferret. Noah loved spending time at his father's office. He liked the colorful walls covered with animal posters. Still, he liked meeting animals most of all. He would stand by the examination bed, next to his father and watch what he was doing.

- "You know, Dad, I want to be a vet just like you. I will finish school so we will work together in this office. " Noah spoke with optimism.

His father just smiled and nodded. He knew he recognized the love in his son, and believed that Noah would indeed become a veterinarian. The boy's eyes would flicker like tiny stars whenever he talked about animals. Whenever he came in contact with them, his face would glow with joy. He liked to sink his fingers in the silky coat of dog's fur and comb them. Cats loved his strokes because the boy had gentle hands. Yes, Noah was definitely born to be around animals. But he had no idea how true that claim was.

The summer break has begun. Noah completed the fifth grade this year. As a great student, Dad let him do whatever he wanted that summer. Noah chose no summer camp or trip. He wanted to go to work with his dad every day and help with the vet's office. Dr. Brown stared at his boy speechlessly, delighted with the idea. He hid a tear that slid quickly out of his eye like a drop of rain and left a wet mark on his face.

Noah's happiness was not over. He went to bed that night excited beyond everything. He got up early, before his father, made him a fresh pot of coffee and woke him up. The two had breakfast and went down the alley to work. The trees above them made a pleasant shade and gave a break from the sun. The birds chatted merrily and followed them to work. Dr. Brown immediately went to prepare the doctor's office for the first patient.

Noah stood by the counter and waited to see who would be the first to come today. Soon the doorbell rang and a roaring sound echoed in the office. Noah saw Rio at the door. It was a wonderful golden retriever due today for a regular checkup. The dog was very happy to see the boy. He showered his face with wet dog kisses and cheerfully hopped around Noah while wagging his tail. Noah dug his fingers into the soft golden hair and ran through it like a comb. Rio was very fond of this sign of attention and expressed his gratitude with a loud bark.

- "Noah, why don't you bring Rio to the exam room. I'll be there soon. " Dad turned and stayed in the waiting room wanting to talk to Sheriff Bill, Rio's owner.

Noah took Rio to the examination room and showed him to climb the table. The boy hummed and rubbed Rio's neck.

- "Who's a good boy? You are, yes, you are Rio! You are the best dog. " Noah repeated enthusiastically.

- "Yes, I'm a very good dog. Scratch me behind my left ear, Noah, please." A voice echoed in the exam room.

Noah froze in a second like an icicle. He turned his tufted blonde head left and right, blinked with piercing sky-blue eyes a couple of times and looked at the dog.

- "Oh ... Did you say that to Rio?" the boy muttered.

The dog let out something that resembled a combination of barking and laughing.

- "Well, who else? It's just me and you in this room. I thought you knew about your gift, Noah." Said Rio and tilted his head to see Noah's reaction.

- "I didn't know I had any gift. So, I talk to dogs? " Noah asked, sitting next to Rio.

- "You talk to all animals. Only special people have that gift. Use it carefully." Said Rio wisely.

Noah pondered on Rio's words. If it's already true that he talks to animals, then he could help them. It's a lot easier to ask someone what hurts him than to question and examine. Noah decided that he would use the best his gift has to offer.

Rio finished his checkup very quickly and it was time for a new patient. Mrs. Collins, an old lady with a beautiful Persian cat on a pink silk pillow, walked into the office. The cat's long, white hair was neatly done and decorated with a little pink bow. It was soft like cotton candy. Noah gently took the cat and brought it for inspection.

- "Hello, Miss Lola, how are you today? Are you sick? " Noah asked, playing the doctor

- "Oh, wonderful! Finally, someone that understands me, thank heavens! That woman brought me here needlessly. Well, I'm perfectly healthy and I'm fine. If only she bought my favorite wet food. These new cat food cans have a bad effect on my beauty. Look, dear boy, my hair no longer has that magnificent glow. And the food tastes terrible!" A cat called Miss Lola complained.

Before he could say anything, Noah's father and Mrs. Collins entered the room. Noah just winked at the cat and whispered:

-"Everything will be fine."

Dr. Brown did a thorough examination and decided that Miss Lola was fine.

"But Doctor," Mrs. Collins began, "she is so sad. She won't eat anything. "

- "Hmm, maybe I could do a couple of tests." Doctor Brown though out lout.

- "Daddy, allow me." Noah said proudly, "Mrs. Collins, have you changed Lola's food?"

- "Yes, I have, young man. I bought her new cans, they are very expensive and of good quality. " Answers proudly Mrs. Collins.

- "You see, I think Lola must have been happier with her old wet food. Even her hair looked better. See how she lost her gorgeous glow."

A silent cry escaped from Mrs. Collin's.

- "Oh no! You're right young man, her hair is in a very bad condition. Oh, don't worry Miss Lola, let's go buy you your old food now. " The owner sobbed.

The cat moaned gently and brushed Noah's hand in gratitude.

- "So, this was something special. How did you know what the problem was? " Dad asked curiously.

- "I didn't, it simply came to me," Noah told one little white lie that wasn't so false, to begin with.

The father-son conversation was interrupted by some noise from the waiting room and a breaking sound of something made of glass. A sharp noise made its way to the examination room and Dr. Brown and Noah rushed forward. A terrible sight welcomed them in the waiting room. The glass table was turned upside down in the corner and all smashed into pieces. Magazines were flying around the room making a rustling noise that disappeared before one dog's bark. It was a big mess of voices from small dogs and big ones. Just behind the door stood a girl tangled in leashes, with a pug beside her, marking his territory with a pungent scent. Two Dalmatian puppies cheerfully dug earth from the flower pot, scattering it everywhere. A cheerful splash of water came from the right and Noah saw a huge bulldog drinking water from an aquarium. Right before them ran a skinny Siamese cat chased by a tufted mixed-breed dog.

- "Oh my God, where to start?!" Dad grabbed his hair in despair. His eyes showed disappointment but also concern about the situation.

- "Don't worry, Dad, I'll handle this," Noah said.

The high pitch of his dog whistle blasted and the dogs stopped immediately doing everything. Somewhere in the corner, the cat kept hissing and puffing on the mix-breed dog. Everyone calmed down and turned to Noah.

- "Okay guys, this is how we do it: stand in line one after the other so we can get your information. You must be quiet. Well, just look at what a terrible mess you made at Dad's office." Noah warned them and frowned at the animals.

The sad bark of dogs echoed in the office as they bowed their heads and formed a line in front of the counter. Even the Dalmatian puppies calmed down and stood still.

- "Oh, this is a miracle!" The entangled girl shouted behind the door. "I thought I would be able to bring them in all by myself. And it was successful until that cat decided it was time to challenge the dogs. Bad, Mimi! " the girl scolded the cat.

But the cat meowed loudly and made a magnificent leap to the high reception desk.

Everyone watched the move in disbelief, and then laughed sincerely.

- "Okay, I see who wants to go first. Let's go, Miss Mimi." Dad brought the cat into the exam room, still laughing.

Noah shrugged and began to untangle the rough straps tangled around the girl.

- "Miss, I will keep them safe, you can go to the toilet to freshen up and wash off the pug smell. You know, it doesn't smell like chrysanthemums. " Noah said softly and gave the girl a charming smile.

She grinned gratefully and hurried to the toilet.

- "Let me know," Noah turned quickly to the dogs, "who needs what?"

The office went bursting with sounds again. The dogs' voices yelled again: sharp, deep, squeaky and joyful. Dr. Brown's office echoed with barking but it felt like happiness.

Noah smiled overjoyed that this would be a school break to remember, a holiday to help beloved animals.

Chapter 6: The Secret Treehouse

In house number nine, surrounded by a tiny white picket fence, and with many flowers in the front garden, it was always fun. Children's screams and laughter were heard every day. It sounded like a happy family was living there. And it truly did. It was made of mom, dad, and twins: brother Alex and sister Ally. The small family was grateful to live in such a place and have a wonderful home. Behind the house were a spacious yard and a small forest with a shallow stream. There were many places where children could play. But still, there are days when every game is boring and the kids need a change.

It was the beginning of a summer break. Alex and Ally already played every game they could imagine. After all, it was too hot to think of anything new. Brother and sister were laying on the floor of their room. Their smart heads worked hard to come up with a new thing to do.

- "I know!" Alex shouted at once, "Some time ago I found a tree in the woods and there was a house on it." Alex said, proud of his discovery

-"Yes and?" Ally asked, not understanding what her brother was saying.

- "Well, we'll make it our secret treehouse! It is in good condition. I just need to fix a couple of holes. " Alex replied thoughtfully as if he was already plotting a plan in his head.

- "Are you going to do it yourself?" Ally asked.

- "No, you silly, you will help me. Come on, let's show you where it is. "

The kids rushed out of the house making sure that their busy mom didn't see them. The day was very hot, but as soon as they set foot under the thick cover of the forest, they relaxed. The path through the forest was well-trodden and clear. It looked like it was being used. They did not walk long when they saw a small clearing and a treehouse. Alex was right: the treehouse was not in bad shape. A couple of roof boards had to be replaced and the rest seemed durable.

- "Oh, Alex, what a great idea this is! With a few new things, this will look like a real treehouse. "

- "Let's get to work. I'm going to find tools and something to fix holes in the roof, and you take everything from the house that you think will help us. "

The children hurried home and began the search. Alex was looking for things through Dad's toolbox. Soon the hammer and nails were in his pocket, a pair of planks stacked on the floor, ready to be carried. He returned to the treehouse alone and in a short time managed to complete all repairs. Ally was still gone. Just as he was about to go to find her, he saw a little girl pulling a baby wagon loaded with stuff to the top. Every now and then, Ally would stop to rest, panting hard, and picking up things that collapsed like a tower on the forest ground. Alex rushed to help his sister.

- "What did you bring? Mom will notice if something is missing. " Alex was worried.

- "Oh, Alex, Mom has no idea we have these things in the house. I brought all this from grandma. She told me I could take whatever I wanted. " Ally replied proudly.

- "Uh, good luck we have Grandma living next to us. Let me help you. We'll finish faster if we work together. "

Two pairs of working hands began to work. Alex was dusting the house while Ally was putting improvised curtains on the windows. Little by little the treehouse got its old glow back. A colorful and soft old rug that Grandma made was covering the floor. Ally sorted snacks and drinks in a tiny table in the corner. All around them were board games, toys, books, and comics.

- "You know what, Ally? The only thing that's missing is our bean bags from the room. Are we going to get them? "

As they were pulling bean bags from home, Mom yelled after them:

- "Will you, at least, tell me where you are going?"

- "Don't worry, Mom. We're here, we're playing close. " Ally replied, reassuring her worried mother

- "Now it's perfect. All we have to do is enjoy our games." Alex said and looked around with content.

- "Hey, Ally, what's wrong? Aren't you happy with the secret treehouse?" Alex asked when he saw his sister's frown.

- "Actually, I think we're missing something else. We miss our friends. It's nice to hang out with you, but I think it would be more fun to invite Jimmy and Missy to join us. "

- "No problem, sis. I'll go get them now. Wait for me, I'll be back fast. " The boy said, and quickly went down the steps of the treehouse that were nailed to the tree.

Ally was right. It was nice to play with her brother, but it was even more fun to share that joy with friends. Jimmy and Missy watched the treehouse enthusiastically. The glow in their eyes spoke of how much they liked the idea of a secret treehouse.

- "Alex, secret means no one, but the four of us, knows about the treehouse?" Jimmy asked curiously

- "That's right, Jimmy. Adults are banned from entering. We should also come up with a password without which we cannot enter. How about 'real friends'?" Alex asked, waiting for his friends.

- "Yes, that sounds great! We are truly best friends! " answered Missy and laughed cheerfully.

The treehouse echoed with the soft laughter that was carried through the forest by the wind. Those voices reached someone who should not have known about the treehouse.

While riding his bicycle, Billy, a bad boy from the street, heard the laughter from the treehouse. He paused and listened where that laughter was coming from. He knew there was a treehouse in the woods, but he was too scared to climb and see what was in it. He was now convinced that the treehouse was harmless since the children were inside.

- "Yes, they are safe in the treehouse," Billy said confidently and headed for the woods.

Twigs twitched at his feet as he made his way through the impassable part of the forest. The sharp thorns of wild blackberries tore his clothes and left red lines on his skin. Billy grunted and passed along, making even more noise.

- "Quiet, friends. I heard some rustling. " Ally said, all serious.

- "Oh, Ally, it's probably some dogs or other animals." Jimmy shook his head and continued to sip on the juice box.

- "Would the animal grunt?" said Ally, pointing her finger through the small window.

- "Oh no, it's Billy. He'll steal our house from us! " said Missy frightened.

- "Not while I'm here," Alex said and pulled out balloons from somewhere.

- "Great idea, Alex. If he tries anything, we'll throw water balloons at him," Jimmy spoke as everyone filled and tied balloons.

- "Well, well... Little children are playing house. Aren't you a little too old for that? " shouted Billy.

It was obvious that the boy was mocking them. He was older than the guys, a ten-year-old, and much taller. He often used to tease friends, throw stones and beat them. He was a very bad boy. He did not deserve to get the treehouse.

- "Go away, Billy, this is our treehouse," Alex said and stood at the door of the treehouse.

- "Oh, really? And who will stop me from taking it for you? " Billy stuck out his tongue, ready to climb the tree.

- "We will stop you. Goys, get your weapons ready! Throw it now! " Alex shouted and threw out the first water balloon.

The balloon ended right on Billy's head, tearing and wetting his hair and clothes. Billy didn't see it coming. He remained frozen in the place and amazed. His feet were heavy as stones. A second balloon immediately followed, and a third, fourth ... Friends threw balloons successfully until Billy bounced back out of shock and began to run. He was wet from head to toe and terrified of their courage.

- "Hurray guys, we made it! We defended the treehouse from bad Billy. " Alex yelled all happy.

Happiness was clear on their faces.

- "Sometimes it's necessary to be a little naughty to save what you love. Sometimes, being bad is the only way to teach others a lesson. Of course, only if they deserve it." Ally said wisely and toasted with her juice box.

"For real friends and our secret treehouse," Jimmy added.

The guys had a lot of fun that day. They went home when it was already dark. Mom greeted Alex and Ally at the door sent them straight to dinner and a bath.

- "Honey, they don't want to tell me where they were." Mom complained to Dad.

- "Oh, don't worry dear. Our kids discovered my old treehouse. Over the years, I have kept it safe. Now they are ready to play in it with their friends. May this summer be as memorable as mine has been." Dad claimed all happy that Alex and Ally continued playing in the treehouse he once loved so much.

Chapter 7: The Land of Magical Creatures

Ever since he found a book on mythology, in his grandfather's study room, Miles has become interested in magical creatures. He was fascinated by page after page that carried images of magnificent beings. He would run his fingers across the smooth surface of the griffin's image and admire his posture. Pegasus, centaurs, chimeras, hippogryphs, and cyclopses dragged him deep into a world of long-forgotten imagination. He stayed in it for a long time. Miles read a lot but studied the beings better with his eyes. He seemed to be able to draw a hippogryph in all his majesty at any time of day and night. He remembered every detail of these unusual mixtures of various animals. His favorite was the hippogriff.

One day, when Miles was drawing creatures from a book, he heard a knock on the window of his room. He raised his head from the colorful drawing and shook it. Did he hear something? A few moments later the sharp sound of knocking on the glass broke through. Miles jumped up and opened the window. A hippogriff flew in front of him. He made a circle in front of Miles, slammed his wings a couple of times, and yelled loudly. The deafening noise pierced the boy's ears.

- "Wow, you are such a loud boy!" said Miles, laughing out loud.

- "And you are one kind boy." The hippogriff replied in a deep voice and bowed in the air.

Miles's face flushed with surprise. He finally realized what was going on. Standing in front of him, better yet, flying, was a real, talking hippogriff. Miles almost thought he was dreaming. He pinched his arm to test it. No, he was awake and the place where he pinched his skin was now throbbing.

- "Are you surprised because I'm talking or because I'm in front of you?" the hippogryph asked.

"Both ..." Miles whispered.

The boy's eyes blinked like stars with excitement. His imagination came true for he saw his favorite mythological being!

-"What now?" Miles asked in amazement

- "Now, dear boy, let's fly. Come on, get on my back and I'll take you to a wonderful place. I'm sure you'll like it. "

Miles jumped cheerfully and clapped his hands. He slipped through the window pane and climbed onto the hippogriff's back. He felt silky, dirty white feathers under his hands. It was so soft to the touch that Miles buried his hands in it and wrapped his arms around the hippogryph around his neck.

- "Hey, do you have a name?" shouted Miles joyfully.

-"My name is Bucky, and now hold tight because we're leaving," Bucky replied, climbing really high.

A small, white house with a red roof was left behind them. Everything from above looked so tiny. The wind carried them, and Bucky successfully slid his wings through the air flows. Miles was not afraid of height or the hippogriff. He relaxed his grip and straightened in the back. He enjoyed the scent of freedom he felt as soon as they took off. Miles' curly brown hair fluttered in the wind. The boy's eyes were closed as he absorbed the magic of the flight.

- "We're landing soon, Miles," Bucky said and started flying down.

It didn't look like a long flight to Miles. They rose high into the clouds and flew for only a few minutes. Obviously, Bucky knew the way. The question was, the way to what?

Greenfields of fresh grass began to emerge beneath them. It was the beginning of spring and the air felt like nature was awakening from drowsiness. As he flew closer, Miles realized that the animals he saw from above were neither wild horses nor cows. They were pegasus and centaurs. The boy cheered enthusiastically and pointed his finger at the peculiar creatures.

- "Bucky, these are pegasus and centaurs!"

- "Yes, Miles, welcome to the land of mythological creatures. Let's introduce you to everyone. " Bucky replied and landed softly in the grass.

Miles quickly got off the back of the hippogriff and ran towards them. The place smelled like spring flowers and freshness, and it felt like home.

- "Welcome Miles," one of the centaurs said, "We called you here because we heard you know everything about us. For a long time, no one visited us. We are forgotten. "

The centaur's brown eyes flashed with sadness, and he turned his head to his flock. Miles followed the movements of his stiff muscles as he moved in front of him. It was a magnificent specimen of its kind.

Bucky joined them and whispered quietly to Miles in the ear.

- "That's Felix. He is not as happy as his name tells him. He is very hurt by the fact that people have forgotten about centaurs and the rest of us. That's why you're here: to tell the world something nice about us. "

Miles just nodded at that. In his little head thoughts were whirring and buzzing like bees. Aside from being excited about the meeting, Miles was very sad about the whole situation. He wanted to help mythological beings. He wanted the world to know how beautiful they were.

- "What ... What can I do for you, Mr. Felix?" asked Miles timidly.

Felix turned and looked at the boy. He lowered his body and bent on the ground.

- "You can do a lot of things, dear boy. You can teach the world to change their minds. You can teach them about all creatures that live on our lands. I'm just taking you to meet the others. "

The boy followed Felix through the crowd. All the other centaurs and pegasus greeted him and looked at him curiously. Miles felt welcome among them. He felt approval and saw hope in their eyes that he would be the one to help them.

- "Our herd is not large. We have grouped several species together to help one another. Pegasus lives in this meadow. The hippogryphs and the griffins are by the lake. Cyclops and chimera live in a cave at the rocks. Everyone has found a place for themselves on this land. " Felix spoke as Miles wandered thoughtfully into the vast expanse they were in.

The meadow was large with trees scattered all over it. There was plenty of sunshine as well as space under the trees that made pleasant shade. It seemed like a comfortable place to live. The hippogriff lake was magical. It wasn't much big, but the water in it glittered like silver. Most importantly, it was clean, rich in fish, and provided refreshments to all species. Miles had already forgotten about worries. He knew deep in his heart that he would succeed in helping these dear beings. Ecstasy took control of the boy. Why wouldn't when he saw a dozen hippogriffs in one place? What a wonderful sight! Everyone rested around the lake, grooming their feathers and looking into the distance. Some would bow to Felix and Miles and greet them with a gentle voice.

The route led the small group uphill to the rocks and cave. It was getting steeper so Bucky let Miles ride on him again. Miles had neither hooves nor claws to climb the sharp rocks. The edges seemed scary as if they were climbing the blades of a knife. Still, the painstaking journey was well worth it. The view from the plateau in front of the Cyclops Cave was incredible. The valleys were on the right and the lake on the left. It was a picturesque sight of fantastic beings.

The cyclops approached them quietly. It was a creature of few words. He just nodded to Miles. Miles saw the wisdom in his eye. It was as if the cyclops had told him that he believed in him. Somewhere beneath them, the chimera stretched out and continued its afternoon nap. Everything seemed so calm in the land of mythological beings.

- "Now that you have seen our home, it is time to go home. Miles, you know everything about us anyway. You know how to transfer knowledge about our species to humans. It was necessary for your smart head to see us in person and to prove to you that you did not believe in our existence in vain. Go now. Bucky will bring you home. " Felix said, looking dark and worried into the distance.

And it was just like that. Bucky carried Miles on his back and cruised through the clouds again. This time Miles did not enjoy himself. He thought anxiously and came up with a solution on how to help the beings.

- "Bucky, do you think I'll make it?" Miles asked curiously.

- "If you believe in something, there is no doubt that someone else will. You just have to show love. I'm sure your friends will love our species too when you tell them what you saw and what you know about us. After all, from whom did you inherit the love for mythological beings? "

- "From my grandfather. You're right, Bucky! "

-"You see. One person already believed in us. Now there are two of you: you and your grandfather. It seems to me like a team that will succeed in everything. " Bucky said and bowed to Miles theatrically.

-"Till next time!"

The hippogriff swung its silvery wings and swiftly flew into the sky. Miles was left to look after him.

- "I'm going to work right away. All my friends will know how magical those creatures are. Everyone will love them as much as I do. I can do anything as long as I believe in myself! "

The boy ran into the house with the hope that only love can give.

Chapter 8: Molly in the Candyland

Like all children, Molly loves candy very much. She loves the chocolate flavor, crunchy candies, and foamy marshmallows. If she was allowed to eat, she would have sweets for all three meals and even snacks. But Molly's mother wouldn't be too happy about that. She makes sure that Molly eats healthy and diverse meals. She gets sweets sometimes as a reward. That makes Molly sad a lot. Her sweet baby head does not realize how dangerous candy can be to her teeth.

- "Nothing should be eaten extensively. There should be a line for everything." Mom always said.

That's why Molly loved to imagine. She would close her eyes tightly, clenching her hands together and imagining that she is far away from home, where candy is allowed. In front of her eyes, she could see milk chocolate waterfalls, a river of caramel, trees full of colorful candies and candied apples, clouds of cotton candy and many more wonders. Those few moments made Molly so happy. Bu then, the real-life calls her back. She finds herself again in a world where candy is limited. What a terrible world.

One day, as she pondered how to find the chocolate bars her mom had hidden, she heard her mother calling her. She rushed to the kitchen and looked at her mom curiously.

- "Oh, Molly, there you are! Liste to mommy, be a good girl now. Mom has to finish some errands. Grandma's in the living room, so stay with her. Watch the cartoons, okay sweetie? " said Mom and kissed the girl on her forehead.

Molly had no problems listening because she was a good girl after all. But like all good children, Molly wanted sometimes to be just a little naughty. The cartoon ended a while ago and her grandmother was napping in her armchair. Molly was bored. She didn't want to watch another cartoon. She needed something else. She needed sweets. This was the perfect opportunity to make run for it since mom is gone. She knew Grandma wouldn't wake up for long. Molly quickly jumped to her feet and ran to the kitchen. The curls of black hair bounced behind her. She stopped in the middle of the room and put her finger on her mouth. The little girl was thinking about the best hiding place for candies.

- "Um, where could Mom hide those chocolates?" asked Molly with a really serious look on her face.

She decided to open one drawer at the time. One by one she opened and closed the doors, finding no chocolates. The kitchen was big, but chocolate couldn't be found anywhere. Molly knew there was chocolate in the house. She just had to find the stash. After examining everything in the kitchen, she decided to check one place she never went to - the pantry. Molly was scared of the pantry because she once saw an ugly, black spider there, and she didn't like spiders. She entered the small room cautiously and turned on the light. There were shelves full of groceries and dishes. Fortunately, there were no spiders, but she saw something that made her smile happy. On the last shelf, hidden in the corner, she saw a box full of her favorite chocolates. She grabbed the box and hugged it. Then she ran to her room so no one would see her. Molly was proud of her catch. She couldn't wait to treat herself to delicious chocolates. She sat on the bed and rustled the wrappers. The delicious milk chocolate melted in her fingers and smelled so tempting. Molly ate with pleasure. The chocolates were among the finest ones. She ate one, two, five, then sat down happily on the pillow and fell asleep. The chocolate-smeared face smiled as Molly sank deeper into her dreams. The search for chocolate had exhausted her, and she needed sleep.

And just what a dream she had dreamed of! Molly woke up beneath a large tree full of fruits. It was a warm day and felt like summer. The breeze played lightly with the grass and whistled a quiet song. The birds joined in that performance and chirped cheerfully on the trees. Molly looked up and saw branches of candied apples above her.

- "Oh, this is weird. The tree that gives candy apples? I see it for the first time!" declared Molly surprised and approached one branch. The tree leaned toward the girl and offered her apple at her fingertips.

- "Thank you, dear tree." Molly quickly grabbed the apple and began to enjoy its sweetness. She liked the sweet part of the red sugar the most. Ok, and she would have eaten the apple if she had nothing else to eat, but a number of treats had just been created before Molly. The girl blinked quickly because she thought she was seeing things. A large river of caramel flowed through the valley. The grass was green and sprinkled with colorful flowers. But these were not ordinary flowers. They were candy flowers. They smelled like real flowers but tasted like the sweetest lollipops. Molly screamed enthusiastically and ran to one of the flowers. His petals were yellow and he smelled refreshing.

- "This also tastes like lemon candy!" exclaimed Molly and moved on to explore.

Caramel river was flowing beside her. Tiny waterfalls were created here and there. Molly climbed one of the many colorful bridges that were crossing the river. No wonder, the bridges were also made of candies! It was licorice, not something Molly would eat. So, Molly decided not to eat the bridges because they would collapse and she would not be able to cross to the other side of this magical valley. And on the other side, there were even more amazing things to enjoy in. A large five-story chocolate and strawberry cake stood in the middle of the meadow. Giant lollipops in every rainbow color were around it. Some strange-shaped machine was producing clouds made of cotton candy. They were sliding gently to the sky. Molly approached them. They were blue and pink and very soft. And they were simply delicious! Satisfied that she has tried a piece of cloud, Molly ran to try the next candy. She nibbled and tried everything she would see in front of her. Pastries, cupcakes, donuts, ice cream, marshmallows ... The list had no end. Everything Molly had ever wished for was emerging before her. Sweets familiar and unknown sprouted like flowers in a meadow. The hot air balloon tossed colorful sprinkles over Molly and the Candyland Valley. The girl closed her glittering eyes and raised her head to the sky. She was catching sweet sprinkles that melted on her tongue.

- "Molly, Molly ..." echoed the valley with a humming voice.

Molly turned around to see her best friend Kelly calling. A smile spread across the children's faces and they hugged each other.

- "Kelly, how come you are here? Isn't Candyland wonderful? I wished for a place to eat all the candies I want and then I woke up here." Molly said eagerly.

- "Yes, the Candyland Valley is beautiful! I'm here because I really love sweets just like you. What should I try first?" Kelly asked interestedly.

- "Oh, let's try the cake. I'm sure we'll like it. Everything tastes so good here."

The girls ran to the big chocolate cake. Its scent drew sighs from the girls.

- "If it smells like that, it has to taste amazing," Said Molly in awe

- "There is only one way to find out," Kelly said and came closer to the cake.

They grabbed its soft chocolate sponge and ate it with pleasure. There was a chocolate cream spread all over their faces. They were happy and didn't mind to be messy from the cake.

The two friends, when they finally got full, lied down under a tree of candied apples. Their pillow was a big donut sprinkled with powdered sugar. It smelled like vanilla and made the girls' dreams sweeter. Molly and Kelly slept well and contented.

Molly's mother stood at the door of the children's room, shaking her head in disbelief. Mom never thought Molly would find the candy stash. She laughed because the picture before her was the sweetest thing she had ever seen. Molly was lying on her bed, smiling, surrounded by chocolates and candy papers. Traces of chocolate were visible around her mouth as evidence of her mischief. Mom picked up the wrappers and candy bars, kissed Molly and left her to sleep. So, what is one mischief from time to time? Nothing! What mattered most to her mother was that Molly was a happy child, and she really was. She will be even happier when she founds out that mom had allowed chocolate almost every day from now. Now, that's a world Molly would love.

Chapter 9: Kitty's Way Home

Tabby has always been a curious kitty. When he came to the house where Andy and Maya grew up, he was just a little kitten. Tabby had no idea that the place would become his home for forever. Mom, Dad, Andy, and Maya gave him lots of love. Tabby grew up and became a happy cat. Every day, the kids would feed him and then play with him. But most of all, Tabby liked to be scratched and petted. When little, quick child's fingers passed through his silky fur, Tabby would enthusiastically purr. He loved Andy and Maya very much. The hours spent with them playing games and cuddling were his favorite. He even shortened his nap time, which was very unusual for a cat.

Andy, Maya, and Tabby lived on a farm. The farm wasn't very big, but it had plenty of animals. Tabby was friends with everyone. The chickens were rummaging cheerfully as he dozed in front of the house. He especially liked cows because they gave the delicious milk that Tabby adored. He liked the ducks too because they were gentle, and they petted him with their smooth, white wings. Still, Tabby's favorite pastime was watching the horses run in the corral. He admired their strength and the beauty of their brown hair.

- "But Tabby, you're a wonderful cat too. Your hair has a lovely gray color and interesting dark lines. You even have the letter M on your head as proof that you belong to Maya. " One day Donald the duck tried to prove it to Tabby.

Tabby looked at him with his big yellow eyes and sighed sadly.

- "Donald, I know I'm a nice kitty. Every cat is a beautiful cat. But I want to be as strong and fast as they are. Look at them! Horses are beautiful! They see vast green expanses of meadows and gurgling rivers. You can feel the wind in the mane as he rushes freely into the sun. Oh, I would love to go on such an adventure at least once. "

Tabby didn't even think that his dreams would come true soon.

As usual, Tabby went to sleep after his afternoon meal. He was welcomed by hot hay straws and felt a pleasant tingling sensation.

"A little nap in the sun would be fine," Tabby thought to himself.

So the cat fell asleep. He slept soundly and oblivious to the environment he was in. He could not feel the hay moving beneath him, or the thump of the wheel against the dirt road. He looked blissful in his sleep. The car was driven far from the farm, to the next neighbors. Andy's and Maya's father dragged some hay and food for his neighbor Jack and returned home on the horse he had bought from Jack. The car was left in the yard of a large farm, with a cat sleeping on it.

It was already night when Tabby woke up. The bowels roared and sent a moan into the world, seeking food and water. Tabby happily stretched and flicked his tongue. He already felt in his head the taste of the cat food that Maya gave him with so much love every night. He lifted his rested body, jumped out of the car and looked around.

- "Um, is it already the end of the day? How long have I been sleeping? " Tabby asked

The cat walked around the farm and stopped cautiously. He sniffed unknown smells in the air. There was no freshly milked milk or the smell of a delicious dinner from Andy and Maya's mom. Oh no, there was no cat food either!

- "Where am I? This is not my farm! " Tabby moaned in horror

The loud clatter of paws on the ground made him turn around. An old dog ran towards him with long ears dragging over the ground. He was very chubby and had a terrible sense of sight.

- "Stop!" The dog shouted, "who are you and what are you doing on my farm?"

- "I'm Tabby the cat and it looks like I'm lost. I just don't know how it happened. " The cat replied fearfully.

- "Wait, wait. Are you that Tabby? Andy and Maya's cat? I really love those kids! Look, their daddy brought this car to my boss. You must have slept on it. " The wise dog assumed.

It looked like a light went on in Tabby's head. His cat's eyes lit up and he agreed with the dog.

-"Yes, exactly! I fell asleep. But how do I get home now? I don't know the way. I've never been out of my farm. Can you help me? " asked Tabby scared

-"Of course I can! I used to be the sheriff's dog. My name is Rusty and I know all about this place." Rusty replied proudly as his saliva dripped down his chin. Rusty missed a lot of teeth, so he sounded funny as he lisped and fizzed.

- "Listen here, cat. I'll walk you to the end of my farm, and then you'll have to go alone. Follow the river, it will lead you to a field with wild horses. After them, go left, towards the forest, but do not enter it or you will get lost even more. Follow the trees and at the end of that forest, you will see a fence. That's the border of your farm. There is a lot to cross on foot, but I believe you will succeed. Once you find your land, listen to your instinct and it will take you to your friends Andy and Maya." Rusty was explaining, and Tabby tried to understand what he was saying.

Fortunately, Tabby was one smart cat. He said goodbye while leaving the farm and thanked Rusty kindly. The little cat's heart was beating fast as he ran. He wanted to get home as soon as possible.

He saw the river very quickly. It was a scene that Tabby could only dream about. The little river came from a distance and cut the valley in two. Its surface was shimmering, and it reflected the setting sun, painting the river red and resembling a red-orange. Tabby had to hurry before the dark.

- "I just want to get to my farm. I don't want to be alone in the dark. " Tabby spoke to himself. He was one brave kitty.

He ran fast, as much as his short cat's legs allowed to. Luckily he had slept and gathered energy for the big journey. This was one persistent cat that did not give up easily. He followed the river without a hitch. He paused only to catch his breath and admire the enchanting nature. The wind was racing with him, passing through the silky coat. It seemed like the wind gave him wings.

It wasn't long before Tabby found himself in front of a herd of beautiful wild horses. Enchanted, the cat approached the animals gently.

- "Excuse me, I just want to take a closer look at you. I think you are magnificent! " said Tabby in one breath.

Strongest among them, a beautiful horse with brown and white hair approached Tabby.

- "You're a cat. What are you doing in the wild? " said the horse boldly.

- "I'm a Tabby cat and I'm lost. I have to get home to my farm before dark. Andy and Maya are definitely waiting for me and are worried. " Tabby answered

- "I'm Pinto and I will help you, Tabby. How about you climb up on my back and I'll take you home. I'm sure your little cat legs will get tired soon. I'm stronger and faster than you." Kindly offered Pinto

Tabby whispered enthusiastically:

-"Yes of course! I would love to ride with you and be as fast as you. "

All the horses laughed. The cat was cute and sweet. The Pinto set off as soon as Tabby climbed on and gripped his mane. The horse ran as fast as a train Tabby had once seen on television.

The wind tickled them, forcing Tabby to relax and breathe in the scent of nature. He could feel the freshness of the night coming and the smell of the trees as they rode past the forest that Rusty had mentioned. Dark silhouettes of trees swayed and played the game with the wind. Tabby would usually be scared, but not now. He was now as strong as a horse and faster than the wind in this race. He felt free and looked like the luckiest cat in the world. Finally, his dream came true. When he tells Donald and the hens they won't trust him.

He felt under his paws that Pinto was slowing down. A wooden fence was noticeable before them, and Tabby concluded it was the fence of his farm. Somewhere in the distance, a thin line of smoke from the house was streaming towards the sky.

- "Thank you very much, Pinto. You made me a happy cat because I got home and I ran as fast as you. " Tabby thanked Pinto with all his heart and the horse bows and rides into the twilight.

The cat feels sad about parting. The yellowish eyes began to fill with tears that Tabby quickly wiped aw with his tiny paw. He remembered he's going home. The cat hurried over the fence and went down the tall grass full of wildflowers. The scents of summer scratched his nostrils and were soon replaced by some others. Mom's dinner and cat's food smelled like a dream and made Tabby hurry home. The wind teased Tabby and carried the voices of Andy and Maya that called for him.

When the little cat appeared before the little boy, all tired and panting, happiness entered the scene. They both ran to hug him.

- "Where have you been so far?" Maya asked through a cheerful, childish laugh

-"Oh, you have no idea what kind of adventure I had," Tabby thought to himself, cheerfully meowing. His dream came true: He was free as the horse and fast as the wind. That night, and the following one, Tabby slept soundly and happily. All was well in this cat's life.

Chapter 10: Jimmy's Good Deeds

In a small town where everyone knew everyone and where everyone loved and respected, there was a boy named Jimmy. Jimmy was just starting school and for the first time in his life, he was faced with the responsibilities that the school carried. The assignment had to be done, the reading to be read, and the boy had to follow instructions in math class. This made it hard for Jimmy because he preferred to be out and about. Like all children, he loved playing with friends. Therefore, he would rush home every day to finish his chores so that he could spend as much time as possible playing. One such day something happened that changed Jimmy.

After finishing all the homework he had for the day, Jimmy ran out of the house and headed to his friend Rex. He was carrying a new soccer ball under his arm. Her white skin with the football club logo glowed in the sun as if the boy had oiled it. It was firm and smooth under the fingers, ready for a full day of shooting on the training ground.

Jimmy quickly arrived at Rex's because the two friends lived very close. He blew up his face and removed his dark, soft curls from his forehead, and rang the bell. The massive white door opened and Rex's mom appeared in the doorway.

- "Oh, hello honey. Rex is not here. He went to the retirement center. It's time for his daily good deed. "

-"Good deed?" Jimmy asked confusedly, scratching his head.

Rex's mom smiled kindly and explained to Jimmy:

- "Yes, a good deed. Rex loves going to the retirement center every Friday and doing a good deed that he thinks will help the elderly. This teaches him to become a good man. He read stories to them last week, and today he went and took them some biscuits he had baked himself. "

Jimmy just nodded slightly and said goodbye to Mrs. Doyle.

- "Good deed ..." Jimmy repeated to himself, "I want to do good deeds too. How could I get started? " the boy scratched his head and thought.

He was sitting on a curb outside his house when a neighbor across the street, Mr. Wilton, pulled out his hose to water the flowers. Jimmy had an idea. It looked like a light bulb had lit up above his head. He dropped the ball and ran to Mr. Wilton, and greeted him kindly.

- "You say you will water flowers for me?" asked the neighbor, surprised, apparently unused to the help of the little boys.

-"Yes," Jimmy proudly replied, "I want to do a good deed and help you. Do you allow me? " Jimmy asked, looking at the old man with his big brown eyes. He looked like a cute puppy begging to get the ball.

- "Oh, of course, beautiful boy. Your help is of great importance to me. Here, you water the flowers and I'll go get some lemonade from the house. "

Jimmy gladly accepted the assignment. The icy water flowed very quickly from the green garden hose and soaked the flowerbed. Mr. Wilton's flower garden was truly beautiful. An irresistible honey scent spread over the whole courtyard, which apparently came from some flowers. The yard looked like a botanical garden. Carefully arranged and tilled beds of begonias glowed in all possible colors. Even Jimmy, who until then didn't even notice the beauty of the flowers, liked the flowerbed very much. Still, he liked the feeling of being useful more than anything. So, he quickly gulped the lemonade and promised Mr. Wilton that he would always be there for him when he needed to water the flowers. The old man grinned, looking at the boy's small, lean body heading back to his house.

But Jimmy paused at the front door and looked down at the porch floor. On the right side was a letter, unopened and addressed to their neighbor, Mrs. Powell.

- "Here's an opportunity to do another good deed!" Jimmy thought to himself.

He quickly jumped off the porch and headed to the left side of their house. Next to them was a small one-story blue house that was always smelling like cake. Jimmy's stomach squeaked and mumbled every time he could smell the vanilla spreading from Mrs. Powell's kitchen. This time was no different. Jimmy's gut was screaming and screaming when he smelled chocolate outside the door. On the sims of the window stood a rich chocolate cake and was cooling. Above it, the lines of hot air swirled.

Jimmy shook his head quickly and knocked on Mrs. Powel.

- "Good afternoon, Mrs. Powell. The postman seems to have replaced the letters again. I found this by our front door. " Jimmy said proudly and handed Adeline Powell her letter.

- "Oh, how wonderful of you to have returned this letter, Jimmy. It made me very happy because this is from my sister. When I think that it could have been lost in the mail and never reach my address ... "Mrs. Powell replied worriedly. And suddenly she changed her face to a smiley one.

- "But thank heavens for you. Want some chocolate cake? It's cooling down, but I think it's ready to be eaten. Just to thank you one more time."

Jimmy grinned like a cat in front of a mouse and sat down happily on a chair in Mrs. Powell's yard.

- "Um, this helping has its other benefits. I didn't know it was so wonderful to help. " Thought Jimmy.

As promised, Mrs. Powell returned to the table with a large piece of chocolate cake and a glass of juice for Jimmy. The chocolate from the cake was slowly pouring over and filling the plate. The cake swam in it and it smelled like the finest bakery. The taste was even better than Jimmy had imagined. The chocolate sponge and cream were sticking to his mouth and sliding down the throat. Jimmy felt like he was swimming in a chocolate river and going to seventh heaven. The taste was amazing, so sweet and uncomparable with anything.

- "This is the best cake I've ever tasted!" Jimmy blurted after eating it and drinking the juice.

- "I'm glad you liked it, Jimmy. Thank you again for returning the letter to me. " Neighbor Powell's warm voice touched Jimmy.

- "No problem, ma'am. If there's anything else you need, I'm here to help. Now excuse me, I have to go home. " Jimmy apologized and politely waved to the old lady who was still looking after him. She then turned her sky-blue eyes and turned her attention to the letter.

- "Mom, I did two good deeds and I was rewarded for it." Jimmy joyfully shouted upon entering the house, telling his mom what had happened.

His mother kissed him gently on the forehead and hugged him. She smelled like a delicious meal she'd cooked for her family. The touch of her hand was like a butterfly kiss; so gentle!

- "My dear boy, I am so proud of you. But tell me why you did it? " Mom asked curiously.

- "I did it because Rex also does good deeds down at the Senior Center. I too want to be a good person and help others. The rewards are great, but I want to help someone water the garden or hang up a birdhouse just for the sake of help. And I'm proud of myself for being good today. I will be tomorrow too, Mom, I promise. " Jimmy said and hugged his mom tightly.

As he promised. Jimmy went to help the neighbors the next day and the next days too. He helped his neighbors mow the grass, clean the garage, find a cat, paint the fence, plant flowers, pick fruit, etc. He became a real little helpful boy.

The wind whirled and flicked Jimmy's hair as he stood swaying and watching his street. He helped everyone in it and felt very proud and happy. He decided to always help the others because the feeling of being of some use to others was wonderful. In his head, Jimmy saw himself as a neighborhood hero and one really good boy. He didn't know what the next day will bring him. But Jimmy did know he'll keep up the good work and complete his good deeds.

Chapter 11: In the toy chest

Every kid loves their toys. They pamper and take care of them, play with them and talk like real friends. Julie loves her plush friends very much. Her room is a real little toy paradise. It is painted pink and white, has a large soft canopy bed and a mountain of scattered stuffed plush on the floor. Julie loves to play there, whether it's rain or sun. Her teddy bear, bunny Jodie, and doll Lisa are her favorite toys. Julie had never heard toys talk, but she talked to them every day. She told them about the past day, what a delicious snack she had, how it was in kindergarten and at Grandma's. It always seemed like toys were smiling and listening with approval to Julie's story. Their bright eyes were refracting and looking so vivid that once Julie wondered if they were real. The girl didn't even doubt that she would get an answer to that question soon.

Today was Julie's fifth birthday. There were many children from the street and kindergarten. Everyone was playing, listening to cheerful songs, eating snacks and laughing. The best part of the day was the big pink cake with five sparkling candles. The kids really liked it. It tasted like sweet strawberries and whipped cream. The cute stained faces of the little ones were happy because they had eaten fine cakes. When the party was over, Julie went to open presents. Colorful boxes, bright decorative ribbons, glittery wrappers tempted Julie to find out what she got from her friends as soon as possible. Among the many sweets and fancy dresses, there were several new plush friends in the form of a cat, dog, penguin, and pony.

Julie was very happy that her colorful companion from the room raised.

- "Mommy, look! Aren't my new friends wonderful? " Julie shouted enthusiastically

- "Yes honey, everyone is beautiful. But you know what? Mom and dad bought you something for your birthday. Come, let's open together. " The mother smiled gently and took Julie by the hand. She led her to a large box wrapped in a sparkling red wrap. At the top was a large silver bow, puffy and with curved ends falling all over the box.

Julie clapped her hands joyfully as she helped her mom unpack the gift. A sigh of delight erupted from the little girl's throat when she saw what it was all about. Mom and Dad gifted her a lovely toy box. The box was bigger than Julie herself. It was painted white with multicolored hearts and flowers, and a beautiful rainbow was drawn on the lid among the fluffy clouds. The gift looked fabulous.

- "Dad made this, honey, and Mom painted and drew on it. We wanted to do something for you. I hope you like it. Now Teddy, Jodie, Lisa, and the others have a place to sleep. " Her mother kissed Julie and stroked her brown hair.

- "My room will always be neat," Julie added and laughed. The melodic voice echoed through the home.

Later that night, Julie went to sleep. She opened her new toy box and started piling it: teddies, bunnies, new toys, dolls, and various cubes. She just left out the doll called Lisa and brought it with her to bed.

- "Good night, dear friends. See you in the morning." Julie said and closed the box.

She cozied up in bed, turned off the lamp, and hugged Lisa tightly. The little girl quickly fell into sleep, tired of her birthday party. Dreams of the past day in which she felt like the happiest girl in the world awaited her.

Not long after there was a whisper and then the sound of a key turning.

- "I told you, Jodie, I know how to open the lock. After all, I'm a wise bear. "

- "Oh, Teddy, you're a stuffed toy." She rolled her bunny eyes and pushed past Teddy's bear. All the toys were piled on top of each other, waiting for their turn. Teddy successfully threw one by one out of the box. When it was his turn, Teddy pulled himself up and flipped over the edge. He fell with a loud thump, got up, shook himself, and turned to the other toys. Glassy eyes looked at their leader curiously.

- "Okay, guys, now that we're all in this together, we can start. Our plan ... "

- "Wait for me!", Cried the doll named Lisa, and escaped from Julie's tight hug. She ran to her friends as her red braids jumped up and down.

- "Like I said," the bear continued looking at Lisa, "Our plan is to make Julie this an unforgettable birthday. It's still not midnight, we have time. Let's go! "

At Teddy's sign, all the toys were scattered around the room. Barbies grabbed tufted pom-poms and repeated dance steps just outside Julie's bed. Bunny Jodie, Lisa, a cat, a penguin and a pony all brought balloons and prepared confetti for throwing. Only Teddy stood and watched the busy toys.

"It's time," Teddy announced.

The brown bear's lumpy body began to climb up the pink blanket on the bed. In a few moves, he was already on top as a true acrobat. After all, he did climb up every night, protecting Julie from evil monsters. He approached the girl and tickled her nose with a feather that flew away from her pillow. The girl frowned and turned to the other side, covering Teddy with a blanket. All the toys panicked to save Teddy, but as a real hero, he dodged and approached Julie again. This time he tickled her nose again and called her with a gentle, bear voice.

-"Wake up, Julie," Teddy said, looking up at Julie with anticipation.

The tiny prickly nose frowned and moved from left to right. The arms looked for dreamy eyes and rubbed them. Still drowsy from the dream, Julie didn't realize what was so strange. Well, it's just her Teddy with her in bed. She looked at him eagerly as if she wanted to ask him what he wanted.

-"Julie," continued Teddy, "we toys want to give you our birthday present." And since we can't buy you anything, we made a small show for you. Come on, guys! " Teddy yelled, and Julie rose in bed and began to look at them with interest. The girl did not say a word, delighted with the scene before her.

Bunny started counting down on the small, colorful drums that Julie got for her last birthday. His wooden sticks echoed in the small, children's room. Lisa joined in on the children's piano, and Teddy stroked with his paws the strings of the guitar they made from things they found in the room. A deep voice touched their ears and spread around them. Julie giggled cheerfully and jumped out from under the covers. Her eyes glowed like candles on her birthday cake. Teddy Bear sang a song about friendship and love. It was a song written by all the toys together for their favorite girl - Julie. Barbie dolls jumped merrily, performing the dance moves they learned from Julia. New toys were tapping and swinging in rhythm. When Teddy's lovely voice fell silent, the last beat of the song fell silent too. The teddy bear bowed deeply and sent a kiss to Julia. The little girl screamed with happiness and grabbed her toys in a big hug. It was gentle and warm as the sun.

- "You are wonderful friends! Why didn't you tell me before that you were talking? We could have had so much fun. " Julie said and began to give small kisses to everyone.

- "Julie, all toys talk. You were too young before, so we didn't tell you anything. From now on we will share all the secrets. We are best friends. Is that right, guys? "

-"That's right!" everyone answered loudly.

- "Julie, we would like to ask you one thing," Jodie said shyly and cupped her velvety ears.

- "Say it, Jodie. You can tell me everything. " Julie replied and gave them a sweet smile.

- "Don't put us in the box anymore. It's beautiful, we like it a lot, but we don't like to sleep in the dark. We can play with the box during the day, but we don't want it to be our bed. We want to sleep with you, snuggled. " Jodie said in one breath

- "Of course I won't lock you up anymore. We are friends and we play together and even sleep together. "

Julie's words were comforting. The toys were sure that the little girl would no longer lock them in the box. No matter how beautiful the outside was, they didn't like the inside of the box. It was a dark and hard place, and Julie's embrace and her soft bed were a much better shelter.

- "Come on, let's go to bed before Mom hears us. We must not let her find out our little secret. " Julie whispered, making a serious expression. She settled into bed, covered, and her toys went up and found a spot on it. Teddy lay down next to Julie and whispered in her ear.

- "Once again, happy birthday, Julie. I hope it has been the best one so far. "

- "Thank you, Teddy. Thanks to you, this was a wonderful day. "

The little glittering eyes of the girl and her friends shut down. They all sailed on a cloud carrying them to dreamland. They dreamed of many games to try out tomorrow. Julie was overjoyed. A warm smile slowly melted on her face as she hugged Teddy and sailed through the land of dreams. "

Chapter 12: How Jackson Saved Winter

Winter wasn't the favorite season for most kids, but snow always managed to save the day. All the kids on the street, at the sign of the first snow, would rush to the hill outside the town to enjoy winter sports. They would grab the warm hats and mittens, pull out the dusty sleds that had been waiting all year long, and take in the endless fun the wintertime has to offer. The snow would rustle and crackle under their feet as they walked towards the adventure. The whiteness seemed resting on everyone and filled the joyful kids with energy. Some were sledding, others were trying to ski, and some were building a snowman and having a snowball fight. There were infinitely many fun activities that could be done to snow. And Jackson loved the snow. Winter was his favorite season. As soon as Jackson saw the first snowflake swinging in the wind and falling on hard, frozen ground, he knew the best days of the year would follow.

It was Christmas already. All the houses on Jackson's Street were decorated with beautiful ornaments. At one, Santa was waving and laughing merrily. On the other one, the same Santa was stuck halfway down the chimney while sleighs with reindeers waited on the roof. Jackson's house had a large snowman in the front yard that glowed in the evening. Jackson especially loved the night when everyone would turn on the lights. They blinked gleefully and played in a familiar rhythm. They were burning for hours performing a game of lights. These colorful lights were the most beautiful when they would cast a glow on freshly fallen snow. But, unfortunately, this beautiful picture was missing this year. December was streaming towards its end, and there was not a single snowflake in the town. Every day, the wind whispered relentlessly, freezing anyone who dared to walk out of the house. It was a harsh winter. Sharp and sad. The bare trees seemed to shake under the gusts of wind and cold touches of frost in the morning. Their bark was hard as stone and the touch so rough. Everything looked so spookily creepy. Jackson didn't like the view outside. Like the weather itself, he was sad too. He was eagerly awaiting the snow and looking forward to a white Christmas. As time went on, he began to think that the snow would not come to their town this year.

It was the night before Christmas Eve. The holiday preparations were moving at high speed. Even though the weather outside was relentlessly cold, the Smith house was very warm and comfortable. A pleasant atmosphere was felt in every pore of the household, while the amazing scent of apples and cinnamon spread throughout the home. Mom cooked delicious apple pies and baked many tiny cookies. The scents mixed in Jackson's nose made his stomach ache for food. He could never resist his mother's sweets. Jackson ate and splashed crisp biscuits with warm milk that pushed the taste of vanilla into his stomach.

- "So, now I'm tired and I go to sleep. Thanks for the cookies, Mom. " Jackson said cheerfully and went to the window once more that day. He checked through the heavy red curtain for the thousandth time that day if the crystal white blanket had covered the ground. Disappointed, he lowered his head when he saw the same icy winter through the window.

Jackson went to bed depressed. He was turning in soft cotton from one side to the other, struggling with sleep. He did not sleep well that night and kept dreaming that Santa was in trouble and that some evil green monster was destroying the winter for all children.

Jackson winced and sat upright in his bed. He was confused in his head and after a few blinks, he managed to wake up. He got out of the warm bed, looked for soft, puppy-shaped slippers, and headed for a glass of water. The boy paused in a few steps. He turned his slightly opened mouth in wonder and suddenly yelled.

- "Aaaah!" screamed Jackson out of his voice.

On his bed sat a real-life reindeer and quietly chewed on a piece of Jackson's comics. His red nose gleamed in the dark just like one of the lights from the family's Christmas tree.

- "What are you doing on my bed?" the boy shouted hoarsely when his voice returned.

- "Oh, you finally woke up. I've been sitting here for hours waiting for you to get up." He flicked his tongue and crossed his front legs in disapproval.

- "You're Rudolph!" Jackson screamed again

- "And you are Jackson!" replied Rudolph in the same tone, "Now that we're done messing around, it's time to get to the task." Responded reindeer strictly

- "What task? What are you talking about? And why am I even talking to a reindeer? Am I still dreaming? " said Jackson, pinching his arm. A red mark stayed on it, and Rudolph took over the talking.

- "First of all, you don't dream, but you already figured that out. Secondly, I am Rudolph the red nose reindeer and I came for your help. Santa is being held by a horrible green monster. He is locked at the top of a mountain in his cave and we cannot save him. That is why there is no snow this year because Santa cannot escape and let it fall. That is why Christmas will fail. " Rudolph uttered in one breath and burst into tears.

- "And how about the number three?" Jackson asked

- "There is no number three, there is none! In fact, there is, you're coming with me right now. We have to save our planet. We must not have Christmas without snow. We must not have Christmas without Santa! " Rudolph was already talking loudly and walking around all nervous.

"I'd help," Jackson said timidly, "but I don't know how." And they shrugged

- "Oh, just come with me and you'll be fine." Rudolph grabs him and pushes him to the window. "You will ride me and we'll be at the North Pole in a few seconds. Just don't tell anyone you rode me, okay? "

Jackson nodded, climbed onto Rudolph and signaled that he was ready to go. He could feel Rudolph's muscles moving at high speed, and he felt the light breeze carry them. As he opened his eyes, he saw them drifting onto the snowy ground, among the colorful wooden houses. They were greeted by merry elves dressed in dark green suits and other gears.

- "We all tried to save Santa," Rudolph began, "Unfortunately, no one has succeeded. The red monster Glump knows all of us and doesn't let us get close. You're small enough to crawl through the tunnel we dug, sneak up on the monster and steal Santa's keys. Are you ready, Jackson? " Rudolph asked.

- "No, but I have to be, for the sake of our Santa, you and all the children eagerly waiting for the snow. Now is the time to be brave. " Jackson replied and slammed his fist against his chest. Elves hollered enthusiastically.

The plan was easy, so Jackson knew he could easily complete it. As he crawled through a narrow, damp tunnel that smelled harsh like the ground, Jackson talked to himself. He decided to do his best to succeed in this mission. He entered the cave quietly, making sure that not one pebble did bounce or the twig burst. He saw the keys left on the table and Glump sleeping above them. The big tufted monster slept in deep sleep. Jackson quickly stole his keys. He hurried over to Santa and silently opened the door. He shook Santa out of his sleep and quietly rustled. Santa realized his savior was there. They both hurried to the exit of the cave. Santa stopped and turned to the monster. There was a murmur, then Santa threw some glittering powder that had fallen on Glump.

In front of the cave was a sleigh with reindeers that took them back to the village. The whole North pole was overjoyed. The elves were jumping gleefully around Santa and shouting his name. Santa laughed and showed them his hand to calm down.

- "My dear elves, I am so happy to be with you again. My return must be thanked by this good boy, Jackson. Thank you, Jackson, with all my heart. You saved me from a wacky monster and now we'll have both snow and Christmas. He will learn his lesson. I made him do only good deeds and to be aware of it. And now, we can continue the celebration. " He officially announced and disappeared among the elves

Jackson smiled shyly and looked around. He helped, he really did. He's a hero. Warmth spilled around his heart, and a smile flashed across his face. Jackson watched the happy fellowship, the colorful countryside, and the beautiful white snow.

- "Let's go, Jackson, it's time to take you back home." Rudolph approached him and carried the boy into the fluffy sky.

Jackson fell asleep that night, finally still. When he woke up in the morning, it was Christmas day, and the city was decorated with piles of soft, glistening white snow.

Chapter 13: How Cody Met Superheroes

Like all his friends, Cody was a boy who loved comic book heroes. He would spend hours and hours hidden behind colorful pages and study new adventures of favorite superheroes. His curious eyes would absorb all the details and create vivid images in his smart head. Numberless times, Cody wondered what it would be like to meet all these heroes. How wonderful it would be if he was part of that family too! He had no doubt that one evening his wishes would come true.

That day, Cody got his pocket money. He ran cheerfully to the comic book store and asked for a new issue of "Mighty Heroes." It was his favorite comic book. He grabbed the thick notebook and hurried home. He wanted to read what happened to Mighty Mike and the others. However, nothing went according to the plan that evening. Upon returning home, Mom announced that they're having guests for dinner, their neighbors the Johnson's. Cody didn't like hanging out with the Johnson's because their son Kyle, who was older than Cody, would constantly tease him and tear up his comics. The boy gritted his teeth at the news Mom had said and headed straight to the room to hide the new comic. He found a place in a forgotten box in the closet and just in case hid it deep behind his clothes. The thoughts in his mind begged the time to go faster.

But time went by very slowly, despite what Cody had prayed for. Dinner passed in a conversational tone between parents, while Cody and Kyle remained silent.

- "Cody, why don't you go with Kyle to your room. Play. I don't want you to be bored with us adults. " Cody's mother told the boys.

- "Okay, Mom," Cody replied not impressed with the idea

Kyle had been in Cody's room many times before and already knew where he was holding the comics and how to run the game console. Like every time, he was mean to Cody. He immediately took a dozen comics and started scattering them. Pages rustled in the air. Some even fell out of their covers as Cody watched helplessly.

- "Oh, what do we have here?" Kyle was intrigued

A colorful notebook was on the desk. It was a comic book that Cody started drawing. The boy had a gift. Kyle was flipping through the pages with so much detail that he thought for a moment that it was a purchased comic. He narrowed his eyes at the appearance of a character that irresistibly looked like him. It was a half boy half-dragon lighting a fire on the playground. The red flames of the fire have colored the page as if it was a real fire.

- "This is me, isn't it?" asked angry Kyle and tossed the notebook to the floor

Cody looked down at his socks. Fear gripped the tiny 9-year-old boy. He lifted his timid head, fixed the black glasses on his nose, and said in a husky voice:

- "Yes, it's you because you're always mean to me."

Kyle was surprised by the boy's confidence. He stood so thin and tiny before him and tried to look dangerous. Kyle laughed arrogantly, ready to make Cody pay for the comparison with the evil dragon. Fortunately, he didn't even manage to swing his arm when a deafening noise came from the closet. It sounded like a train was going through the room. The bed began to shake and things started to fall off the wall. Suddenly, like an explosion, something exploded out of the closet. Clothes flew all over the room. Cody and Kyle were behind the desk, clenching together in fear. A bright yellow light flashed from the closet and blinded the boys. There was a bang of footsteps and soft music in the background that gave the impression of euphoria. Five superheroes emerged from the thick smokescreen. They all stood side by side and looked around.

- "Um, yes, I told you well, Mighty Marcus. This room is too small to hold us all. " The man in a bright blue suit concluded

- "The room is not too small, but we all went through the closet. Who else tries to fit the portal into the closet?" Answers strawberry blonde man

Cody's eyes flickered and his jaw dropped almost to the floor. In front of him, in life-size, stood his favorite superheroes: Mighty Mike, Mighty Marcus, Mighty Misty, Mighty Mia, and Mighty Dog. They were all dressed in their suits and wore capes on their backs. They were exactly the same as the author had drawn them and Cody imagined in his head. They oozed with strength and power and encouraged confidence.

Kyle watched silently what was happening. He assured himself that he was only dreaming and no comic book heroes appeared in front of him from the closet of one Cody Emerson.

- "What about him?" asked the curious Mighty Mia.

- "Let him go, he's shocked, and he has no idea who you are," Cody said and quickly closed his mouth surprised of his voice

- "I suppose you know who we are?" Mighty Dog spoke to him

Cody swallowed the saliva with a big "gulp" and answered with a faint voice.

- "Of course I do. You are Mighty Heroes, my favorite comic book characters. "

- "Comic book characters? Ah, it's just a mask. We are real superheroes! Comics are just portals that can get children to us if we need them. " Mighty Mike, the main superhero, said proudly.

- "Honey, it sounded like you were in trouble. Did this guy here make you problems? " Mighty Misty asked gently.

Everyone looked at Kyle who just rolled his eyes and collapsed into unconsciousness.

- "Oh, such a coward. No wonder we had to come to save you, Cody. " Mighty Marcus scoffed

- "But how will you help me? I still can't believe you are real. My heart is pounding with so much joy! " shouted Cody a little louder than he wanted.

All the heroes laughed heartily, as Mike spoke.

- "We are real, of course, and our problems are real. We came to you for two reasons. The first is to help you get rid of this bad boy Kyle. And the second is to help us fight the evil monsters that have occupied our secret hiding place. We saw that you know our world very well, but also that you have a very rich imagination. We just need someone like you. " Mike said and held out the boy's hand.

- "Are you coming with us or not?" he asked again

Cody walked over and stood thinking.

- "What am I going to say to Mom?" he asked like a really good kid.

Again, all the heroes laughed at his remark.

- "Don't worry, we'll be returning you on time for school and homework. School comes first. You have to study hard to become a true superhero. " Mike winked and the group went to the portal in the closet.

Then they synced all their watches and grabbed their hands tightly. Mike squeezed the button on his watch and they disappeared. They flew through space and time when the portal dumped them on the top of a tall, glass building. Images of the glittering city were changing in front of Cody's eyes. He realized that they are in the same city, only now the city was upside down, like in a mirror. Thousands of warm yellow lights flashed through the night. Somewhere in the distance, the trumpets were yelling and the dog barked relentlessly. The sounds of the wild city carried through the night, making the noise that ears were so accustomed to. Cody stopped and listened to the sounds of the Mirror City. He inhaled the deep smell of the fresh night that rolled over them. Stars in the sky glittered like silver belts and buttons on Mighty Heroes' costumes. Cody turned and saw that the five heroes were watching him. They looked so magnificent standing in the wind. The long black and blond hair that belonged to Mighty Misty and Mia swirled around them with blue silk coats. Mike and Marcus stood with their arms rested on their chest. The strength of their muscles was reflected through the costume's material, and Cody thought they were certainly the strongest people in the world. Might Dog ran to Cody cheerfully. He waved his yellow scruffy tail at Cody. Even the dog believed that Cody would become a great superhero. He just needed to grow up.

The boy watched as he tried to remember every detail of his favorite heroes, fearing he would forget this happened. This scene etched into his memory.

- "So, are we going to save our hiding site or not?" Mike asked, winking at Cody

The boy's face was illuminated with a wide smile. He ran into a big group hug with his superheroes determined to defeat the villains side by side with Mighty Heroes.

Chapter 14: Charlie's night at the supermarket

Charlie was always a clumsy boy. As soon as he opened his eyes in the morning, his troubles would begin. He would spill a bowl with cereals, step on a dog, break a plate, trample flowers, and it would not be even midday. Everything Charlie was doing was not of bad intent. He was simply a clumsy boy that was out of luck. The things he experienced were often scenes you could only see in movies. He remained locked out of the house three times and had to wait for his parents to come home. Once he fell asleep on the bus on his way back from school and went as far as five stops away. On the way back it rained and Charlie ended up falling in the puddle. The neighbor's dog chased him every day just to pull him by the socks and pull his pants off. A lot of things in Charlie's life went wrong. And while he was fighting misfortune, everyone was saying Charlie was naughty. What an injustice! Charlie decided to show everyone what a naughty Charlie really looked like. He came up with a plan and was very proud of it. He expected that after this try, everyone would realize that Charlie had never been bad before and his clumsiness would finally be apparent.

It was a Friday night, and after school, Charlie headed to the mall with his parents. It was time to get groceries and the whole family, made of mom, dad, brother Johnny, sister Jessy, and Charlie headed to the market. Charlie always hated these shopping trips. They were annoying, so he decided to find his mom and tell her he'll go home to sleep. It was getting late and Charlie was very tired of school. Mom easily accepted Charlie's lie and continued shopping.

The boy fled to the furniture store and hid in a massive closet. He decided to wait for the store to close and then set off on an adventure. At home, he already made the basketball balls look like he was sleeping in his bed in case mom checks on him. In his head, Charlie laughed happily at his plan. He stayed sitting in the closet for a long time. Fortunately, he chose a roomy one so he could lay down and fall asleep.

When he opened his eyes again it was still dark. He stretched out muffling moans. The cracking of his stiff bones echoed the market since he was sleeping on the wooden floor. He stepped carefully on the hard and cold marble floor. The lights all over the market were dimmed, but it still was visible enough when his eyes got used to the dark. Absolute silence ruled the space. There was no one there. Charlie whimpered enthusiastically and jumped up in the air. He slid across the floor to the stairs and, taking two at a time, ran to the night guard. He knew it was his friend's grandfather. As he suspected, the old man slept soundly.

- "Huh, good luck Jeremy told me his grandpa doesn't hear a thing. " Charlie whispered

He ran to the lined bikes by the entrance and grabbed the one he liked best. The beautiful blue bike was even better than he had imagined. He circled on it through the aisles and between the rafts as if on a race track. He paused in front of the candy department and clapped his hands.

- "This will be fun!" he laughed happily

The candy bars he loved the most were gone from the shelves in a matter of seconds. The boy's fingers were sticky with milk chocolate, while a smudge was around his mouth. Charlie enjoyed the silky chocolate texture and divine taste. In a blink of an eye, Charlie felt like he was in seventh heaven. He had all the sweets and snacks available that he could eat. The boy tossed foam marshmallows into his mouth, tore fruit rolls with sharp teeth, and crunched mouthwatering lollipops. He had no idea how long he'd stayed in the candy department, so Charlie decided to pack his pockets with all sorts of things and move on further.

The first stop was the department where the trampolines were. Charlie always wanted one. He climbed cautiously on a rubber pad that was cold to the touch. He swayed slightly and jumped up. The trampoline responded by sending Charlie high and welcoming him into a soft embrace. The market echoed with Charlie's laughter. Charlie giggled and grunted loudly. It was one of his favorite things in life.

As much as the trampoline party was fun for him, Charlie had to admit there were so many more to explore. His list included:

- Switching clothes on men's and women's dolls in the clothing department

- Playing with animals from the pet shop

- Enjoying unlimited ice cream at the cafe

- Watching a movie in a movie theater

- And of course, he plays with all the toys he might like in the shop

Charlie decided to start with toys. Still, he was a kid who wanted to have a lot of fun. He ran as fast as his feet were carrying him to the toy department. He let the robots walk, controlled the cars with a remote, kicked the balls as far away as he could, stacked the tallest dice tower, fired his water guns at the shop's advertisements and had a lot of fun.

- "Oh, this is better than when I was home alone and watching TV all day!"

His heart jumped from happiness as he made a run to the pet shop, his favorite place to visit at the Market. Charlie was very fond of animals, but he had no pets because of his mom's allergies. This was a unique opportunity to pet all puppies and kittens. The cute critters were sleeping when Charlie walked into the pet shop. The puppies were in a pay pen and at the sign of Charlie's smell they woke up. Why wouldn't they when Charlie smelled of chocolate and sweets. The tiny faces of the golden retrievers looked like they were smiling at Charlie. The boy sat among them and hugged each one of them. Happy puppies gave Charlie countless wet kisses. Charlie really enjoyed the touch of their soft, almost fluffy golden hair. It was his favorite breed of dog. Tired of playing with puppies he was overwhelmed with joy. He rested his lean body on the floor, grabbing one of the puppies by his side. Other chubby puppies settled around Charlie and they fell asleep together. Before he fell asleep, Charlie decided that hanging out with puppies was better than trampoline and candy.

He was awakened by his mother's gentle hand. The sun was breaking through the curtains and playing a game of light on the floor of the room. Charlie abruptly jumped out of bed and looked around. He was in his room. But how this happened when he was with puppies a while ago?

- "M-Mom, where am I here? Am I not in the mall? " the boy asked confused

Mom just patted him on the back slightly:

- "You didn't, Charlie, you slept in your room the whole time. You probably dreamed. After all, we're going to the mall tomorrow. "

- "But Mom, I was really there. I was a bad boy! I ate all the candy, cycled through the market, jumped on the trampolines, played with toys and petted the puppies. I did it to prove to you what it means to be naughty. I'm not naughty, I'm just clumsy. "

Charlie frowned, made an angry face, folded his arms across his chest, and kicked his leg hard with a loud thump.

- "Um, that would be very bad if you did. But you're still a good boy. True, clumsy, but very good. That's why you would never hide in a mall and do all that stuff. " Mom said calmly

Charlie decided it was really all a dream. Now that he thinks about it, a night at the mall didn't sound like a good idea. Being naughty is not good for anyone. Therefore, he decided that he will be the best boy from now on and will make sure that no accidents happen to him. Who knows, maybe he'll get the dog he wanted so much! After all, everyone knew that mom's allergy was only to cats. Charlie thought to himself and laughed softly. The room remained bathed in light until the walls of Charlie's house echoed with the morning laughter and the sounds of the conversation during breakfast.

Chapter 15: A day at the beach

Summer finally lazily dragged itself into town. After a spring that only gave them rain and splattering of the ponds that year, it was the turn for warmer days to kick in. The sun was burning from above every day, sending hot rays to the ground, as if to make up for the rainy days. Everything in nature received the much-needed energy and seemed to come to life suddenly. The flowers in the gardens showed everyone their brightest colors. The birds sounded like they were holding concerts every morning. Their kind voices were inviting people to join in. Everyone was in a better mood, but the kids the most. The little children were looking forward to the summer and could hardly wait for days to get warmer. This meant going to the beach every day because the town was right on the seashore. Two sisters, Lilly and Luna, were eagerly awaiting their first beach trip that year. Mom and Dad took the day off from work and promised their daughters to a full day of fun. The small, family-owned, red-colored car was packed with things like they were going on a seven-day trip. A colorful rainbow umbrella was peering through one of the windows, a trunk full of beach stuff could be seen in the background. Even rubber floaties with unicorns and flamingo birds rode proudly on the roof of the car. The family was excited and could not wait to get to the beach. The ride there was not long. Enough for Lilly and Luna to sing to their parents a few songs. Their sweet voices echoed in the car as mom and dad laughed happily. It was a picture of a real, idyllic family.

The beach spot was hard to find. It seemed as if the whole town that day had decided to freshen up in the sea and enjoy the hot sun. Lilly and Luna screamed with joy when they saw the blue sea and the yellow sea of sand in front of them. All over the sand, there were colorful umbrellas, floaties, and towels. The light beach balls rolled over the sand under the gust of wind. It was one of the most beautiful beaches in that part of the country. The sand was fine like salt and had the prettiest light color. Residents took great care of the cleanliness of the beach and water. The sea gratefully gave in return the refreshing water temperature and fun waves which raised from time to time.

Lilly and Luna settled down with their parents by the sea. Dad put on the big colorful umbrella and Mom spread the deck chairs on the sand. Soon both girls were in their costumes and smeared with sunscreen. They didn't wait for Dad to come with them but immediately ran to the shallows to play. Daddy came quickly and brought them their toys: a bucket, tiny shovels, and small rakes.

- "Girls, how about we make a sandcastle," Dad asked cheerfully

Lilly and Luna snapped in surprise and clapped their hands. They took the shovels and started filling the cans to help Daddy. He has already started building the sandcastle. Little by little the towers of the castle were rising up and it was growing in height. It was almost as tall as Lilly! Daddy pulled the flag out of somewhere and placed it at the last tower's top. Mom came and brought small pebbles and some shells to decorate the castle. It looked perfectly good as if it had been drawn. However, the sandcastle didn't last for long. Unfortunately, there was a big wave that came suddenly and covered them all. The water sparkled in contact with the sand, tickling the little family and bringing their precious castle back to the sea. Only a formless mass was left embellished with the remaining stones.

- "Don't be sad, girls." Mom said as she pushed their wet brown hair from their face, "We'll make a new castle later, a little farther from the water this time." She comforted her little girls

- "Let's go into the water. Today is the day we teach Lilly to swim, right? " asked Dad with a smile

Lilly moved slightly towards the water as if she was afraid of swimming.

- "Don't worry, you'll make it. Swimming is quite easy. " Luna whispered, reassuring her sister.

Luna had been a good swimmer for a long time, so she joined her dad to teach Lilly.

Lilly entered the water gently. She could feel the cold sea caressing her skin and slowly rising its level as she went deeper. Lilly's skin became all bumpy from the cold water.

- "Hey, Lilly, you look like a hedgehog! " Luna shouted a joke and touched the prickly skin of her sister's hand.

Daddy took Lilly and held her in the water. Lilly's belly was leaning on daddy's arms as the floated.

- "Relax your body, honey. You need to be calm in the water and without any panic. Feel how comfortable the sea is and how it cools you. Run your hands slowly through the water. You feel how smooth it is like your mom's favorite silk blouse. "

Lilly just nodded.

- "Remember Lilly, I'll be there for you. You just move your arms and legs and push yourself away. You see, just the way Luna does. " Dad said, pointing to his older daughter who demonstrated swimming.

- "Uh, Luna's doing it so easily. She looks like she's a mermaid, not a girl. " Lilly thought to herself

- "Don't worry, you'll be fine." Encouraged her Dad

Little by little, Lilly began to move through the glittering surface of the water as Dad followed her. She cut the water with movements as sharp as the grass Luna and she used to play with. The legs followed those movements and pushed Lilly away. She looked like a little frog while trying to swim.

- "You're doing it fine, honey!" yelled mom from the beach and put her head back under the umbrella.

Luna clapped at her sister playfully and cheered. A sense of determination was born in Lilly as she moved faster and further through the beautiful water of the sea. She reached her sister and quickly turned around. Dad wasn't even near her! Lilly felt like she could swim to the end of the world. She made it! Her little heart pounded even happier because she successfully mastered swimming lessons. Lilly was swimming now all by herself. The fear was gone and it looked like it had never been there. There was a bunch of sounds in her ears, echoing as if she was listening to a seashell. Those sounds were a feeling called pride which made the little girl's heart warm.

The two sisters swam together to the beach and hugged each other as soon as they came out of the water. They jumped together in the air, carried by happiness: one because she had learned to swim, the other because her sister had fulfilled a wish she had for a long time.

- "Come on, guys. I have a reward for all of you. " Mom invited them under the umbrella.

She pulled four ice creams out of her portable cooler and shared them:

- "One for Dad because he was such a great teacher. One for Luna because she was so passionate about cheering on her sister. And, of course, one for Lilly - our star of the day. Congratulations sweetheart, I knew you would learn how to swim today. " Mom said and kissed her baby girl warmly

The ice cream was like sent from heaven. It was the best thing to have on this hot day. The chocolate on the stick smelled so invigorating. And just the taste it had! The sweetness of the icy reward spilled over their fingers and mouth making the girls look muddy but still overjoyed.

The day was perfect. Obstacles were defeated, they received a delicious reward and they had a lot of fun. What more could a small family want?

After freshening up they all went into the sea together and played with the ball. Cold droplets of water fell across their faces and sparkled in the sun like diamonds. But, the children's smiles were the prettiest. They glowed. They were more valuable than the precious stones themselves. The following laughter was just a symphony that was expanding across the beach and floating into the ears of every listener.

Chapter 16: Sarah and the Fairies

Ever since her mom read her first fairy tale, Sarah believed in fairies. She dreamed that she too had one that would fulfill all her wishes. Because of this, Sarah only loved stories about fairies. This night was the same as the rest nights. She lied tucked into her warm bed as Mom was reading the story. With the dimmed light on the walls of the room, heroes from the story appeared to her. The pictures were lined one after the other. It seemed like Sarah was there with them. Mom's gentle voice rocked the little girl and sent her to the land of dreams. The book closed with a slight rustle. The rocking of the chair stopped. The floor creaked slightly under Mom's light step as she kissed her baby girl for a good night. Sarah looked so peaceful. She hugged her plush bunny in her sleep and smiled slightly. Her soft blond hair spread across her pillow. The little, blue angel slept peacefully, carried on the waves of a story she heard. They say that the stories we hear have a lot of influence on our dreams.

It was still night and Sarah was sleeping. Old Tomcat lazily stretched on Sarah's bed. There was absolute silence in the house, and then there was a whisper. With three loud "poofs" Sarah's room flashed with three colors: red, blue and green.

- "She's sleeping." A tiny voice said in surprise

- "Yes, and she looks like an angel." Added the other one

- "It's midnight, what did you expect? She needs to sleep because she's only five. " Adds the third voice.

There was a murmur, hiss, and a rattle somewhere in the room, and three lights flashed again. Three fairies stood around Sarah's bed and looked at her curiously. Each of them had a magic wand in their hands at which end a real star sparkled. They wore long ball gowns in red, blue and green sprinkled with sequins. The silver hair was tufted in a beautiful bun and combed so it looked like cotton candy.

Suddenly, the girl's eyes opened widely and all three fairies huddled together, confused.

- "I knew you existed!" Sarah whimpered and sat down quickly on the bed. In that sea of whiteness and softness, she looked like she was sitting on a cloud.

The fairies quickly recovered and the red one approached Sarah:

- "So no need to introduce ourselves? Do you know who we are? "

-"Of course I do," Sarah replied importantly, "you are good fairies from my stories." You're Betty, "pointed to the red one," blue is Letty and green is Kitty. You came to fulfill my wishes! " clapped Sarah with pleasure

The fairies looked at each other and the eldest, Betty, spoke, fixing her red, sequin dress.

- "Yes, we are good fairies. But we can't fulfill your wishes until we teach you something. " Betty said calmly and went on, "each of us will fulfill one wish for the next three nights if you are a good girl and complete the tasks. Well, you can't just get three wishes for free. You have to earn them."

Sarah looked at the fairies in astonishment and then asked:

- "If I'm good then can I ask for anything I want?"

-"Of course. All we can do for you. " The Fairy in the middle, Letty, nodded.

"And now, the tasks," Betty said seriously, "To get my wish, you have to help mom make cookies tomorrow." Do you think you could do that, Sarah? "

Sarah answered affirmatively. She loved watching her mom bake cookies and now was the opportunity to go ahead and help her.

- "See you tomorrow then, Sarah. Save us some cookies. " Kitty said, and all three fairies disappeared as they came: with one big poof.

Sarah hardly fell asleep. She was bubbling with excitement. In the morning, she asked her mom to make cookies, which she enthusiastically accepted. The cookies were very tasty. The house smelled of vanilla because of them. They were sweeter than sugar, with soft crusts and a silky cream that slid down the throat fastly.

That night the fairies reappeared. Sarah surprised them with saved cookies and Betty, Letty and Kitty ate them happily.

- "Now is the time for your wish. Are you ready, Sarah? " Betty asked

-"Yes, I am. I want a puppy! " snapped the little girl

The fairies looked at each other significantly and Betty replied:

- "Tomorrow morning, when you get up, a small white dog will come to your door, hair tufted and soft like cotton. You and your mom will adopt him. " Betty then waved a wand that blew silver dust sparkles that fell on Sarah. This meant that the wish was fulfilled.

Indeed, the next day she was greeted by a small, white puppy. After some begging, Mom softened and now they had a small pet. As much as playing with the dog was fun, Sarah didn't forget the task. Letty had asked her the night before to do something nice for Mom. Sarah thought hard and then decided to do a few little things that Mom would appreciate. She cleaned her room, stacked toys, wiped dust in the house, picked up fresh daffodils from the garden, loaded washing machine, and watered her houseplants. After all that, she made a refreshing lemonade and called my mom to come and show her what she had done. Her mother was overjoyed at Sarah's good deed.

Later, in the evening, the girl excitedly recounted a day in which she was very tired, but also very valuable. The fairies smiled contentedly, revealing a series of teeth as white as pearls.

- "What can I do for you, Sarah?" asked Letty

- "I want my mom to get the job she always wanted. She keeps saying that she gets very tired at his job, so I wish Mom wasn't so tired. I want her to be happy and have more time to play with me. " Sarah replied and looked at the fairies with her big blue eyes. She looked like a porcelain doll.

The fairies were expecting Sarah to ask for a new toy, a bunch of candy or something the kids were looking for. They were surprised by Sarah's modesty. Letty smiled kindly and said:

- "Tomorrow your mom will get a call for a new job. That's what the three of us promise. "

The fairies have fulfilled their promise this time. Mom got a phone call early in the morning that made her smile all day long. She got her dream job. Sarah was overjoyed but couldn't forget about her third assignment. She had to help someone she didn't know. This was very difficult because Sarah knew everyone in her street. She was sitting in front of the house on the stairs thinking about what to do. She also wanted a third wish because she was saving it for something special and important to her. As she sat so sorrowfully in the street, a truck drove by and a car followed. Then came some people who carried the furniture and a small family with a girl Sarah's age. They moved into the house next to Sarah's.

- "That's it!" The little girl blurted and ran to introduce herself.

She met a little girl with long black hair and even darker glowing eyes called Jenny. She helped her bring toys into her new room. In just a few minutes the little girls became friends and were already giggling gleefully. Sarah was thrilled because she had completed the task and met a new friend.

When she told the fairies at bedtime what happened, they were clattering with happiness over Sarah.

- "Real friends are sometimes found in people you never thought about. You really are one wonderful girl. " Betty sniffed and wiped her small, pointed nose with a handkerchief in the same shimmery red as her dress.

- "And now is the time for your wish." Announced Kitty.

Sarah thought for a long time what to look for. There were lots of ideas and of course she thought of fun toys and sweet treats. But Sarah wanted something that was much more important to her. She nibbled on her lip red like raspberry and stared at one at a time as if she's afraid to ask them. With a loud sigh and a gasp, Sarah dared to say what she wanted.

- "I want a dad, my dad. I want him to live with us again. Can you make that happen? " the girl asked pleadingly

The fairies gathered together and discussed. What Sarah was looking for was a big deal. Only three of them could fill it.

- "Sarah, I need the help of my sisters Betty and Letty for this wish. Since you are such a wonderful child and are only looking for what's really important, we will be happy to fulfill your wish."

Kitty swung her wand, spilling the stardust and sequins all over the room again. Shiny dresses of red, blue and green rustled as the fairies swirled around. They threw a speck of magic powder at Sarah who immediately fell asleep. The fairies went as they came: with that loud poof sound. The children's room remained quiet and peaceful. In a white fluffy soft bed, Sarah dreamed of beautiful dreams. In the morning, when she got up, her dad's smiling face stood in the living room.

Chapter 17: Billy and the Pirates

When his dad promised some time ago that he will get his own room, just the way he wanted it, Billy never dreamed it would look this great. It wasn't very big, but it was enough for a seven-year-old boy. Its walls were painted white with light blue waves drawn on them. The carpet was the same blue color, fluffy and restless as the sea itself. The shelves were painted white and served to keep Billy's books and toys. But the special thing about his room was the bed. It was a dark wood bed that consisted of two parts. Billy slept on the ground floor. Then he could climb up the stairs to a small gallery that had a mast and even a steering wheel. There was a pirate's flag on the side, and a small, torn sail fell on one side of the bed. It was the right room for a young boy obsessed with pirates.

Billy was very fond of everything that had to do with pirates. All his books and picture books were about them. He loved the sea and the freedom it gave. Most of all, he loved pirate ships. These magnificent sailboats glided the sea and cut it like a sharp blade. They seemed daunting in comparison to the ordinary fishing boat that Billy's dad had, and on which Billy often played pirates. Billy wanted to be a pirate. But, unfortunately, he knew it was impossible. His books taught him that the age of the pirates was long gone. He was only able to see them on the pages of picture books and imagine that he was there. Sometimes we need to be careful about the things we want. Maybe they will come true, no matter how incredible they sound.

It was the first night Billy had to spend alone in his room. The boy was not afraid. Besides, he could not hide his excitement. He adored his new room and firmly promised everyone that he would spend most of the time there. His dad read him a good night's story about the famous Captain Tiger, who was terror and tremble of all seven seas. Billy listened enthusiastically to the story and imagined every scene in his head. Of course, he knew each of his books by heart, but every re-reading would reveal something new to him. He rediscovered the legendary worlds that provided new adventures in which Billy was the hero. Dreams soon visited Billy and Dad put the book on the shelf. He tucked in his little pirate and kissed him goodnight.

Billy's head spun left and right. He seemed to be having restless dreams. No one could guess what the little boy dreamed of. Like most of his dreams, this one was about the sea. Sometimes Billy would dream of sailing a pirate ship. But this time, he dreamed he was the captain of a pirate ship.

The boat was a real big black sailboat. He called him Black Beauty. The ship had a large deck that was cleaned by sailors every day. The sails were whole, white and big enough for Black Beauty to sail the fastest of all pirate ships. The pirate flag was proudly displayed on the mast as a sign for all ships who is operating this sailboat. Billy stood proudly at the steering wheel and watched his crew. He was the youngest captain in pirate history. He managed to collect so much treasure he didn't even know where to hide it. His crew followed his every move with awe. All that Billy did not see, his parrot Polly saw for him. A green, screeching bird was standing on his right shoulder, giving out information. Billy didn't allow any problems on board. He considered himself a good captain who would never exploit his sailors. Still, stories were circulating on the ship that Billy was vicious and was stealing treasure from other ships. This was by no means true. The story spread like a vicious lie by his great rival Captain Johnny. Johnny was older than Billy for several years. It was an evil person stealing treasure from other pirates. No one loved him or even his crew. Everyone was secretly figuring out a way to get rid of Captain Johnny. Eventually, they turned to Captain Billy. He always had creative ideas.

Billy thought for a long time and made a plan to solve the problem called Captain Johnny. He couldn't just go in a regular battle. None of Billy's cannons could hit Johnny because he was hiding out as a coward. As soon as Black Beauty would reach Johnny's Punisher ship, Johnny would open all the sails and escape. Billy didn't want to go after him. He didn't want an unfair fight. So he came up with an ingenious idea. All the pirates were supposed to meet on the big sunny island in the form of a treasure chest that July. It was an opportunity for pirates from all over the world to meet and hang out.

Billy arrived first. His crew was setting up a table at the beach with a feast. Slowly, the other pirates began to arrive. Billy whispered the plan to everyone. Everyone agreed with him. It was obvious that they will finish with Johnny today.

The island was full of pirates when Johnny arrived. He looked arrogantly at all the pirates and acted like he was the strongest and best of them all. Just then Billy got up and began a toast.

- "Ahoy, pirates. We gather here to celebrate the rich year behind us. If I'm not mistaken, this has been one of the most fruitful years. May your sails always be wide, the wind fast, the water warm, the bellies full and treasure chests buried safely. "

All the pirates shouted and toasted to Billy, who continued.

- "As you know, one of us must always be better than others. I have to be fair and admit that Captain Johnny is that person. Captain, we have a present for you. " Billy said, pointing at two members of his crew carrying a huge suitcase. It was so big that Johnny could easily fit inside it. The sailors were huffing, puffing and sweating as they lowered the chest in front of everyone.

- "Captain Johnny, get in the chest and we will shower you with gold and jewels. You will receive a great deal of treasure from all of us. "

Johnny's eyes widened in wonder. He was delighted with the proposal. The greedy captain ran and entered the suitcase as soon as possible, spread his arms, close her eyes, and waited for the rain of treasure. He stood there motionless for a few seconds, and then a great roar came. The sailors closed the lid of the suitcase, left the keys inside, and tied the suitcase with rough ropes. With great effort, they pushed the chest to the ship. Johnny was grunting and screaming all the time. He threatened Billy and the other pirates as they enjoyed a feast on a sandy beach.

They left Johnny on one island. It was a beautiful place with a lagoon full of delicious fish. The forest on the island had food in abundance. Johnny was secured and far from all, at the end of the world.

So Captain Billy became the legend of all seven seas. All the pirates respected him because he saved them from the naughty Johnny. Billy was now happily traveling with his Black Beauty. He could freely enjoy the beauty of the sea, the clear water of the waves on the ship and the wind that gave them the power to the sails. In the evening, when everyone fell asleep, Billy would go out on the deck and watch the shining stars flicker and glare at the sea. He was grateful for the life of a pure-hearted pirate.

The small body moved in the bed and opened its dreamy eyes. A boy named Billy looked around the room and saw that he was lying in his bed. Of the pirate stuff, he had only his own ship-shaped bed. The whole adventure was just a dream. So the boy turned to the side and went to sleep hoping to dream again of the Black Beauty and the open sea.

Chapter 18: Adam's New Friend

Adam was always a good boy. He helped happily mom and dad, played with his younger brother, went shopping for his grandparents and studied well. He was a real good guy. Nothing was too hard for Adam. He did everything with a smile. Everyone loved him because of his positivity. He was also a favorite of the teachers at school and had many friends. Everyone wanted to be friends with Adam. One day the news in the classroom was that a new student was coming to school. Adam's classmates were looking forward to making new friends and hoping that the new student would come to their class. At the beginning of the first hour, the lovely Mrs. Newton, the headmistress of the school, walked into Adam's classroom and announced that they were getting a new pal.

- "Please, children, be very kind and help Jason feel welcome. I trust you will get along well," said the principal, inviting Jason to come in.

There was a whimpering sound of metal and a hushed clatter of wheels. Jason, a boy in a wheelchair, entered the classroom. He looked the class with his warm brown eyes smiled shyly, and lowered his tufty dark head. It was clear he was scared of the new environment. Miss Meadows, a teacher in this class, kindly placed Jason in his place by the window. In an introduction, that was so quiet that only a few heard what he said, Jason revealed something about himself. He said he came from the capital because his dad got a new job. The boy also had a brother and a sister. He loved sports and drawing. He sounded like a perfectly normal boy, which he was. However, the other students looked at him cautiously. It was the first time any of them had seen a child their age with a disability. The children did not know how to approach him. Everyone except Adam.

As soon as the bell rang for the lunch break, Adam walked to the first bench by the window. He stood in front of Jason, offered a hand and simply said:

- "Hi, I'm Adam."

- "I'm Jason, nice to meet you." A new student replied, quite surprised that Adam had approached him.

- "Shall we eat lunch together? Today, it's pizza is on the menu and the whole school smells delicious. Oh, by the very thought of it my belly already growls." Adam blurted while grabbing his stomach theatrically

- "You wanna eat lunch with me?" asked Jason, as if he didn't hear it right

-"Yes, why not? This is an opportunity to show you the school. It's pretty fun for a school." Adam said, laughing at his joke

- "The thing is, I changed a dozen schools, and in none of them, I came across a friendly welcome. People avoid me because I'm handicapped. They don't realize I'm a kid, just like them. "

Jason looked very sad and Adam decided he had to cheer him up as soon as possible.

- "That's terrible!" Cried Adam, "Those children have no idea how wrong they are. You're a boy like any other. Why should they avoid you because you're in a wheelchair? That's very rude of them." Adam concluded wisely

Jason was very pleased with what he heard. His pale face got color again and a smile was lingering. Jason laughed, revealing two rows of perfectly white teeth under metal braces.

- "You are a very good person, Adam. Can we be friends?" asked Jason, hoping Adam would agree.

-"Of course! That's why I came to you. " Adam said, inviting the boy to follow him.

They entered the school cafeteria, which was bathed in the sun. Children's laughter was piercing the walls and spreading outside school. Everyone was chatting lively, happy that it was finally lunchtime. Adam waved before Jason and showed him where the cafeteria line starts.

- "You see, pizza is the most delicious food here. It has a thin crust that crunches when you bite into it. The ham is so delicious and mouthwatering. And cheese! Oh, the cheese will make you jump out of your skin! " Adam spoke with great enthusiasm

The boys ate their pizza peacefully and enjoyed every bite. Indeed, the pizza was as good as Adam described. Jason tapped loudly on his stomach, murmuring that he could hardly wait for pizza again.

- "It's every Tuesday," said Adam, "Until then, we'll have lunch again tomorrow. Tomorrow is fish and fries. And you'll like it. " Claimed Adam

The first day of school went amazingly well. Even Jason's mom and dad listened with delight to what happened at school. Parents were used to Jason being sad and hateful in every new school. They sincerely hoped that the boy had finally made friends and that he would love school.

The next day, Adam waited for Jason outside the school's entrance. The two friends said hello cheerfully and walked to the classroom. They were chatting about math homework when Joshua stood in front of him. He was an older student who often teased the younger ones. As soon as Adam saw him he realized there would be problems. He swallowed the sound of saliva and prepared to confront Joshua.

- "Hey, kid, who's your friend? Does he have a license to drive here? " Joshua asked, laughing at his ugly joke

- "Joshua, it's really wrong to joke with someone just because he's in a wheelchair," Adam informed him

Seeing that Adam had no intention of messing with the new student, Joshua changed his plan. He blushed, turning his face red like a pepper. He was breathing fast and blowing out his nose, furious that Adam had reacted that way.

- "You dare to oppose me, you ... you little ..." Joshua shouted rudely, and headed for Adam, ready to beat him.

Adam quickly stepped out in front of Jason to protect his friend. He was a very brave boy, ready to sacrifice himself for friendship. Fortunately, someone shouted that the headmistress was arriving and Joshua was on the run. Along the way, he tripped on his own feet, slamming hard against the floor with a loud thud, and fled the scene as soon as possible.

Of course, there was no sign of the principal. Adam and Jason started laughing out loud after the initial shock. The cafeteria echoed their merry, childlike laughter. Tears flickered from his eyes, wetting the school uniform. They barely made it to the classroom.

Joshua was no longer approaching them. He realized that Adam was there for his friend and that he would fight. It was one problem less. The other problem was their classmates. No matter how genuinely good Jason was, other kids from Miss Meadows's class didn't approached him. Only a couple of girls came to meet him and that's it. Adam was very sorry to see his friend being rejected every day. So he decided to take one bold step.

One day, when everyone was leaving for lunch, Adam jumped up and closed the classroom door with a loud jolt to keep them all there. He looked quickly around the class, his eyes wide open.

- "Don't worry, I'll be short. I have something to tell you. Ever since Jason came to our class, you've all been acting really bad. You're not friendly at all! Why? Jason is a wonderful boy. If you just gave him a chance, you would see what I was talking about. So what if he is in a wheelchair? Miss Meadows has always taught us not to judge others by their looks and to value people with disabilities. After all, Jason plays basketball better than we all do together." Adam said, looking glaring the class.

No one, not even Jason himself, expected this speech. They all bowed their heads. They looked like a set of culprits awaiting sentencing. The classroom was eerily quiet. Not a fly could have been heard there.

- "So what do you say? Will you give Jason a chance? " Adam asked, looking up at the shy boy.

- "Yes, we will Adam!" everyone shouted loudly

They quickly formed a row in front of Jason and introduced themselves politely. The warm touches of the children's hands filled Jason's heart with happiness. He was delighted with Adam's move and overjoyed that classmates finally accepted him. Like on the line, boys and girls switched, putting out their soft hands and sharing sweet smiles.

Adam stood to the side, watching the scene. He had a new best friend and a bunch of old ones who finally overcame all their prejudices. He was proud of himself for leading them to do so. After all, it doesn't matter how anyone looks. What matters is how people behave and what they carry in their hearts. A pure heart and sincere intentions make magic called friendship.

Chapter 19: Bella's and Star's Adventure

When she was a little girl, for her fifth birthday Bella got a horse. Bella couldn't even think what that horse would mean to her. Years passed by, seven of them, and Bella still had her horse. She called her Star, because of the large white spot on her forehead that had the outlines of a star. It was a beautiful black mare, with shiny hair like the darkest night. Under the hot sun, that hair was shining and glistening. Star was delicate to the touch like cotton buds. She had warm black eyes, glittering like the stars she was named after. Star was a racehorse. Her strong muscles stood out on a body that was ready for all-day running. That's what Bella and Star did every day. As soon as daybreak, Bella got up and had a quick breakfast. Mom would pack her sandwiches, and the girl would head to the barn. Star waa always there, waiting for her, leaning against the barn's door, ready for Bella to saddle her. Star never complained about Bella riding her. She would look curiously at everything the little girl was doing and readily waited for her departure. Fortunately, Bella was an excellent and experienced rider. After all, she has been riding since she was five years old. She held the reins firmly in her hands and told Star where she wants to go.

That morning was no different than the previous ones. A quick breakfast, then a hike with Star. Bella decided to go up the north side of the ranch that day, to the mountain. She had heard from her mom that the herbs she was using for her famous balms were growing there. Bella decided to surprise mom and pick something up for her. Determined in her intention, Bella turned Star to the north and showed her the way. The mare neighed and blew out air loudly. She put all the strength she had into her legs and took the path Bella had shown. The day was beautiful. It was late spring and warm enough to stay all day outside. The ranch's green pastures stretched endlessly. The fresh grass was just bathed in dew. The breeze puffed pleasantly, bringing with it the scents of mountain flowers and fresh air. The ranch cows were already out and munching the grass lazily. The bells around their necks made a melodious sound that echoed the pastures. Bella and Star watched the colorful cows curiously as they rode between them with a light trot. It was nice to see other animals enjoying an endless source of food. As soon as the first pasture passed, Star started running faster. She rode as fast as her legs carried her, and Bella allowed the mare to spend her energy. The girl squinted and gave Star the freedom to ride. She believed in Star that she would not take her to the wrong side. She breathed in the fresh air a sign that they were already close to the mountain. It smelled invigorating and clean, like when her mom puts laundry on the wire to dry. Bella spread her arms and let the wind flow through her fingers. Long brown hair flew behind her like a cloak. The scene looked like it was from a movie. Bella felt so powerful as if she could conquer the whole world.

She had been riding for about an hour when a fast river began to appear on her left. It descended from the mountain and cut the valley in half with its deafening rapids. The sight in front of the little girl and her mare was spectacular. A magnificent mountain appeared on the horizon. The snow was long gone so now the sharp edges glowed with the bluish color of the stone. The mountain was not too high, but it was enough to make Bella feel stunned. The little girl rarely came to this place. She was here last time a couple of years ago, and since then she forgot everything she has seen before. The river was chilling. The mountain dominated the view. The colorful wildflowers were so pretty. It was a beautiful picture. Everywhere the view went, there were colors. To Bella, it looked like all the possible colors of the world blended in one large carpet. oh, but the smells were a whole other story! The delicious smell of the honey mixed with the different scents in the air. The bees were buzzing noisily, collecting pollen for their honey. The whole meadow roared cheerfully and emitted vibrancy.

Bella gets down off Star and takes the reins beside her. The mare was picking grass and enjoying a refreshing taste. They took a light step towards where the river, separated by a rock, formed a small well. Bella freshened up and showed Star to drink water. They needed energy that day. She pulled out a small, sharp knife from her backpack and set off to cut herbs. She knew exactly what mom needed and which ones were rare to find. She would always watch her mom make balm so she learned all about it herself.

- "It will be a wonderful surprise for Mom. Don't you think, Star? " she turned to the mare and giggled sweetly

Star swung her head up and down as if she understood what Bella was talking about. The two of them understood each other like true friends.

Bella got busy. She cut the plants, separated the flowers from the leaves, from some of them she took only the roots and packed everything in her backpack. Textures were changing in her hands: from delicate petals to velvety leaves and rough roots. Collecting the herbs took a long time. The sun was now high in the sky and frying mercilessly. This was one of the warmer days announcing the quick arrival of summer. Somehow, as soon as spring takes its toll, summer pushes past it and brings along unbearable heat. It is a sign for all creatures who want warmth to come out from their hiding places. Bella knew she always had to be on guard. Here and there she knew how to find snakes sunbathing on rocks, so she would just bypass them. Today she looked around every few moments as if expecting something to happen. Bella's instinct was right. She just finished picking the plants, when she turned around and saw Star nervously stepping back in front of something. The mare gnarred and puffed. She shook her head from left to right, rising on her hind legs. As glorious as the Star was on its hind legs, Bella stopped admiring it because she realized they had a problem. She quickly took her backpack and ran towards Star. The scene she found only confirmed her suspicions. The star cried out before the snake which was moving lazily towards her as if hypnotizing the horse. Bella recognized her poisonous rattle. The eerie rattlesnake sounds scratched their ears. Bella's blood froze in the veins. She had a split second to react, so she grabbed Star by the reins and stepped as calmly as she could backward.

- "No sudden movements ..." the girl repeated in herself

The snake paused for a moment and began to wiggle its tongue as if searching for where they had gone. Bella seized the opportunity and jumped on the Star and made her run as fast as she could. Bella didn't dare to look back. She made Star go faster as the mare's muscles trembled with force. The spit was flying all over as Star ran to rescue both. They were very lucky. Bella's heart was pounding madly. It sounded like it was in her ears. The eardrums threatened to pierce every second. In record time, they crossed the mountain's valley and pastures. When they arrived in front of the corral on the ranch, Bella took Star to get water and sat down exhausted in front of the house. Mom came out and saw that her little girl was upset.

- "What happened, honey?" said Mom and stroked Bella on the wet hair that was now a tuft of brown mane

-"Don't worry mom," Bella said when she recovered breath, "it's okay, nothing happened to me or Star. We had a rattlesnake encounter under the mountain, so we quickly escaped from there. "

-"Oh! But why did you even go to the mountain? " screamed mom worriedly

At that moment, Bella pulled out a backpack full of herbs and handed it over to her mom.

- "I heard you ran out. We must not allow ourselves to be left without your balm. I just wanted to help. " Bella answered and lowered her head

At that moment, an indescribable warmth poured into her mother's heart. It was impossible to describe with words how much love mom felt for Bella. She hugged her daughter hard, kissed her soft forehead and whispered in Bella's ear:

- "You are one incredible child. Thank you very much. But please be careful and don't go there anymore. "

Bella just squeezed Mom harder in response to her plea. Mom hid one tear. She was very scared of what Bella had told her, but at the same time, she was immensely happy. Her adorable little girl was just fine. That was only that mattered.

Chapter 20: Leilani's Adventure in the Jungle

Living on a big island was a beautiful thing. Leilani appreciated every moment she spent on Sun Island. She lived there with her family made of mom, dad, and brother. Few children can brag with a sweet little house near the beach, and Leilani was one of them. Every morning she was awakened by the murmuring waves hitting the sharp edges of the rocks. The sun would sneak into her room like a thief as the wind swept through the airy white curtains. Leilani's room was in the attic of the cottage. She climbed the wooden steps, bound by lianas. The whole cottage was the work of her father, but the attic was decorated by Leilani herself. The big mattress was so soft that the little girl thought every night that she slept on a cloud. Through the ceiling window, she would see the twinkling of stars and through the open door the vast openness of the ocean.

The days on the island passed in a relaxed atmosphere. After all, in this place, the sun was shining almost all year long. Rare were the rainy days. Because of this, the island was named Sun Island. Thanks to the nice weather, Leilani spent every day at the beach. She was a great swimmer. As she glided gracefully through the water, turtles, colorful tropical fishes, and sometimes dolphins would swim beside her. The whole island and life on it were idyllic. However, sometimes things get into the routine and everyone needs a change.

Leilani didn't go to the beach that morning. The previous day she had spent all day on it, swimming, sunbathing, collecting shells, and making sandcastles with her younger brother. She needed something more fun today. Her brother, Kai, went shopping with her parents that day. The girl was left alone at home because she was a big 12-year-old. She sat in front of the cottage and looked thoughtfully into the sea.

- "Um, what could I do today?" Leilani let out a quiet whisper

Her dog Lilo seemed to respond to her with loud barking. It was a small mix-breed that always followed her footsteps. Leilani adored that tufted creature, his brown eyes, and soft hair.

The idea flashed like a lightning strike and Leilani hit the forehead theatrically. Lilo looked at her in astonishment, tilting his head to the left.

- "Well, how could I not remember that! Let's go deeper into the island today. I have always wanted to explore the old path of flowers."

She quickly jumped to her feet, slipped on her leather boots, packed her backpack and grabbed a small machete. It was important to be prepared to defend against any danger in the jungle. Lilo ran gleefully after her as Leilani made big paces toward the north of the island, where the famous jungle entrance, the path of flowers, is located. The trail is named after numerous tropical flowers that attract bees, butterflies, and hummingbirds with vibrant colors. The whole time she hummed and vibrated along with the sounds that were made in the flowers. Leilani especially loved the hibiscus flowers in bright red. She loved their delicate petals that would caress her face when she stuck a flower behind her ear. Her long black hair created a beautiful contrast with the color of the flower.

Leilani paused, picked out a flower for her hair, and turned to see if Lilo was following her. The puppy sniffed curiously at the flower bushes, exploring the various scents.

The path through the flower-filled path was short but brought some rest to the eyes. As she stepped deeper, the trail narrowed, greenery intensified, and sunlight diminished. Trees towered above Leilani's head as they made a tunnel that led deeper into the jungle. Leilani walked with caution. She was a very brave girl, but she was still afraid of running into a snake. She loved all animals, but the cold and smooth skin of the snake made her cringe.

Somewhere above her, a bird grunted and the parrots on the branches screamed. The whole jungle was echoing with a brawl of birds that seemed to be competing which would be louder. Leilani whimpered loudly, urging Lilo to follow her step. She didn't want her dog to go too deep into the jungle. The road was getting narrower and the greenery was getting thicker. It was time for the little girl to use the machete. Sharp strokes cut the lianas, which interrupted and intertwined one part of the course. Leilani skillfully handled the machete. She had it ready in case of an emergency. The purpose of today's adventure was to find the field of orchids. She, just like her mom, loved those flowers very much. She wanted to find one that was unique. It was soon mom's birthday and Leilani thought it was a great opportunity to find a special flower.

She had been walking the road for a long time and looking for orchids. Noon was long gone. Just as she decided to go back, she saw a turn to her right that she could make in a few strokes with her machete. She made her way quickly through the plants and remained silent on the scene she saw before her. In front of her was a small valley, no larger than a portion of the beach in front of her house. It was full of the orchids she wanted to find so eagerly. All the colors in the world seemed to have gathered into that small space. Leilani opened her eyes in wonder and screamed enthusiastically. Lilo ran past her and paused to see what the little girl had found. Leilani couldn't decide which orchid was prettier to her. She decided to surprise her mother with beautiful purple flowers. Thank heavens she kept an eye out every time mom took care of her plants. Otherwise, she would not know now how to successfully separate the flower and bring it home.

Leilani was pleased with the job. She looked into the little piece of blue sky that was visible through the thick canopy, and she decided it was time to go home. The journey was long and strenuous for an already tired little girl. Lilo, on the other hand, enjoyed it. That dog had the energy he was drawing from everything around him. He bounced joyfully, snooping curiously around him. Suddenly he buried himself in the place. He lifted his right paw into the air, sniffed some strange odor that pinched their nostrils, and let out a hoarse bark. Lilo felt the danger. Leilani also stiffened in fear. When a wild boar came out on their way, Leilani screamed in terror. It was a dangerous creature, not at all nice to the eye. Lilo didn't feel frightened at all. The courage in him came to the surface and it seemed as if the puppy had grown bigger suddenly. He threatened with a growl at a wild boar that was blowing and grunting, ready to fight. When Lilo released his voice, it sounded like a roaring lion in the jungle. The whole place echoed with Lilo's barking. The puppy barked and foamed with saliva, boldly approaching the wild boar. The boar, whether from fear or astonishment that a small dog was barking at it, shook her head and fled back to where it came from.

Only then did Leilani breathe out of her lungs with a hiss. She grabbed Lilo and ran toward the house. Now was not the time to admire the flower path. She wanted to find her home as soon as possible.

- "The jungle was a dangerous place after all," Leilani concluded and squeezed her little dog's body tightly in gratitude.

She left the orchid on the table for mom and when she asked where she got it from, she just shrugged.

Later that night, Leilani couldn't sleep. She got out of bed and went out on a fresh night. The sea air smelled astounding. She sat down next to Lilo and stuck her fingers into his soft neck. She was just grateful that the day ended well and that she had Lilo, not as a dog, but as a best friend who always kept her back. After all, that's what friends are for.

Conclusion

Bedtime stories often come with valuable morals. Kids learn that greed can get them into dangerous places, like maybe into a witch's oven. This might protect them from the lure of many predators that hide in broad daylight.

They can learn to stay on track like the turtle who won the race. I am a parent. I have seen how greatly these bedtime stories can affect children. These are the very values they can carry throughout their lives. So it's important that the morals we transfer into them, are well thought out.

I have also seen how bedtime stories can often furnish children with great problem-solving skills. They tend to make your child attentive and mindful. These are among the many effects that I have seen result from bedtime stories. But mostly, it's surprising to me how effectively moralizing they can be. This has driven me to form a set of stories that I can use to educate them morally. This motivation has made me struggle, and somewhere along the way, it became my passion.

So, finally, I decided I should write a book that would satisfy this purpose and my passion.

Finally, if you found this book useful in any way, a review on Amazon is always appreciated! Wish you all the best!

Lightning Source UK Ltd.
Milton Keynes UK
UKHW021235051220
374629UK00012B/866